Introduction

Thank you for placing your trust in the concepts of the *Palmer 60/40 Golf Method*. There are many outstanding instructional books for golf—as Bob Hope famously said, "The problem is they all say something different!" Golf can be at once thrilling and beautiful, maddening and frustrating. I hope this book will serve as a system that allows you to discover a way to simplify and improve your golf swing while increasing your consistency.

The book is written to you personally—by that I mean it should read like you and I are having a conversation in much the same way as my students and I converse during a lesson. Moreover, the book is organized in straightforward, yet comprehensive chapters that include all of the elements and concepts of each particular swing including fundamentals, swing concepts, drills, and exercises.

Hopefully this will allow you to work through all of the thoughts related to one swing without having to flip back and forth between different chapters. Each chapter can be read as a stand-alone discussion or lesson on that topic. I hope you read the book in its entirety first and then come back to specific chapters when necessary. The organizational pattern should allow you to return to different sections if you are having trouble with an area of your game during the season. Also, I should mention that the ideas and techniques described in this book represent one way of improving your golf. There are many other worthy and useful strategies that deserve your attention and study. After working with countless students over the years, I have come to the realization that golfers are unique and each player needs an instructional program tailored to best compliment his or her physique, aptitude and abilities. A great teacher uses bits and parts of the body of work, of course, anchored around the key fundamentals of the subject to construct the best plan of action for a student. This book contains many ideas that undoubtedly will be helpful to most students but there are other ideas or somewhat contrary ideas that might also benefit certain golfers.

The instructional concepts are intended for golfers of any age, ability level, experience level, or gender. This edition of the text is intended specifically for left-handed golfers. In other words, all of the notations are directional for left-handed golfers. Also, many references are listed with generic terms to designate a side or part of the body such as front or lead versus back or trail instead of being repetitive with the words "left" and "right." Left-handed golfers will associate references of lead or front with right and trail or back with left.

Golf is a deceptively difficult game—especially given the fact that the ball is not moving as it is in almost all other sports. However, the rotary nature of the golf swing causes much of our body, as well as the golf club, to be moving in many subtle ways. Therein lays one of the truly difficult aspects of golf—returning the clubhead back to the ball at an effective impact position and synchronizing the body's movement in a dynamically athletic way that delivers maximum speed and power into the shot while minimizing unnecessary lateral and/or vertical movement of the body and controlling the club face's impact position with the ball to produce an accurate strike.

Another underrated aspect of golf that adds to the game's difficulty is that we encounter totally different shots on every hole throughout a round; literally every shot is unique. Other than while we are on the putting green, we change clubs constantly, rarely using the same club for two consecutive swings. Thus, we swing clubs of different lengths and feels, from different lies, distances and situations, and on holes that produce unique challenges every time we approach our next shot. The preparation time we have requires many calculations and decisions before we even start the golf swing.

Then we are challenged to execute those concepts in a correct physical manner and in a relatively short amount of time. These challenges are some of the underlying reasons why golf is such a difficult game.

LEFT-HANDED GOLF SWING FUNDAMENTALS

THE PALMER 60/40 GOLF METHOD

WARNE PALMER, PGA

SUMMIT CLASSIC PRESS
AKRON, OHIO

TABLE of CONTENTS

Before and during the writing of this book, I deliberately avoided watching instructional golf television programs and reading any writings on the subject. Like most golfers, I have a collection of my favorite instructional pages clipped from magazines over the years as well as a small library of books that I respect and that hold the most meaning to me. My ideas for this book, obviously, have been accumulated from years of playing, reading, teaching and listening, and I wanted to make sure I expressed the concepts in this book totally with my own thoughts and in my own words.

Hopefully, you will find the *Palmer 60/40 Golf Method* to be an effective way to simplify the playing of this wonderful game. The fundamentals presented in this book have been developed over the years while instructing students. Their feedback and improvement has aided me tremendously. This system will help you increase the number of solid, dare we say great, shots you hit during a round.

One thing that brings all of us back to golf is the incomparable feeling we have when everything comes together in a shot, and we feel the ball explode effortlessly off the clubface with such a solid impact that the ball flies perfectly on line at our target. It's that rare but unequalled experience that ultimately keeps us playing golf.

Sure, we also enjoy the friendships, the games, and the inherent competition of doing our best against par, but the quest to improve our skills and expertise is one of the chief motivations that keep us searching for personal answers to the riddles of golf.

Our pride drives us to stay on the road to self-improvement—the desire *to get better* and to strive for that elusive *perfection* we know only exists in occasional glimpses. My wish is for this book to help you gain more skill and knowledge in your golf and increase your enjoyment of this ancient and magical game—I hope you profit from the lesson!

Part One: The Five Swings

Let's get right to it—not all full swings are the same. In fact, the five groupings of clubs we swing fully *all* require slightly different techniques to be used effectively. That being said, there are threads and concepts that connect all full swings. Those commonalities will be discussed fully throughout Part One as we work through the five distinct swings.

Full swings are best thought of as technical, trained and practiced movements. This is the one place in golf that we want to attempt to be more robotic rather than instinctively athletic. The reason why is simple—we want to *repeat* these swings as similarly as possible again and again while playing golf. Most of the time while we play, we will hit a series of shots imperfectly and as a result, we are faced with the task of making corrections in our full swings literally one shot after another. In order to be able to *self-coach* ourselves through the swing flaws and changes we need to make before the next shot, it is incumbent upon us to learn *our own* swing characteristics and fundamentals well enough to be able to quickly analyze what caused the shot we just hit to fly off-line, curve or determine simply what went wrong in our swing that caused the ball not to be stuck as solidly as we had planned.

This kind of analysis is best accomplished by building our golf swing through a series of technical movements and concepts that we deliberately attempt to repeat over and over again, week by week, month by month and year by year. It is complicated by the fact that we are not programmable machines, and that we are constantly changing physically as we continue to age. Progress will never be in a straight, ascending trajectory; we will experience good days and bad days. However, the more self-awareness and knowledge we gain regarding our golf swing, the better equipped we are to improve and make positive adjustments.

As we go through the five groupings of clubs and swings, please keep this idea in mind—balance your thinking between the technical and the instinctive aspects of the golf swing. Our missed shots will usually be a result of the combination of these two factors not matching-up perfectly during a swing. Sometimes, the identification of the swing flaw we just made in the previous swing and the necessary correction we should make prior to the next swing can be best determined and processed in the technical realm through an analytical, intellectual approach. But on other shots, we can instinctively *feel* what we did wrong during a swing and determine the appropriate correction we should make. So, the more we learn about our own golf swings and tendencies, the easier it will become to fix mistakes during a round.

For example, if I hit an approach shot that lands short and left of the green, I need to identify the cause of that short/left miss by quickly examining the possible issues in a cause and effect manner.

Did I select the wrong club for the distance? Was the shot not struck solidly? Did I misjudge the wind or was the green elevated, which adds effective yardage to the overall distance? Did cold temperatures have an adverse effect on the distance the ball flew or was my body too far in front of my arms and hands causing the club not to transfer optimal energy into the shot at impact? Was my swing plane too steep or too flat? Was the club face open at the impact position because my grip was too neutral or did I quit on my follow through rotation toward the target? All of these thoughts are possible causes of the short/left miss and unfortunately there are still others.

The point of this example is not to overcomplicate, excessively analyze or become obsessive over a slightly mishit shot, but rather to point out the initial step we should engage in following a swing that produces a less than satisfying result. We start with this analysis in order to avoid the same problem on our next approach shot swing.

Oftentimes, identifying the cause is not a perfect science. But, the more knowledge we possess about the fundamentals of the golf swing and the more we know about our own golf swings, the greater likelihood we have of selecting the most plausible swing flaw that created the negative result on the previous shot. The second part of the self-coaching process is to determine what adjustment, if any, needs to be made before the next full swing.

Whether you decide that the error was caused by a technical flaw or an instinctive physical or mental error, it helps to identify the most likely cause of the mistake by quickly computing the possibilities and prioritizing the most likely option(s). These thoughts will logically connect the undesired result to the adjustment(s) required to fix and avert the same problem going forward. Having a mental checklist of your common swing tendencies and the resulting causes and effects in your full swings can be vital to you avoiding a negative tailspin in your ball-striking and confidence.

Knowing the technical fundamentals of each of the five full swings as they relate to *you* and *your* five swings is of paramount importance as a golf course forces you to change from one swing type to another while playing. Executing proper swing mechanics in succession requires a delicate balance of emotional, mental and physical control. This is an extremely challenging and often overlooked aspect of playing golf at a very accomplished or high level and hitting as many quality shots as you can during a round of golf.

Chapter 1 Wedges

Most golfers find their wedges to be the clubs they use the third most often while playing only following their putter and their driver. The importance of wedges lies in the sheer variety of uses they provide to golfers. Wedges are employed to negotiate a vast array of situations, lies and distances from full swings of approximately 100 yards to shorter scoring shots from sand bunkers to the most delicate, finesse-filled greenside chip, pitch, lob and flop shots and everything in between.

Key Points for Wedges: Q & A

How many wedges should I carry?

Unless you hit your driver and other full swing clubs exceptionally long distances, you should carry two wedges beyond a pitching wedge. Most manufacturers design iron sets with four degrees of loft between each iron; for example, a typical 6 iron has 31 degrees of loft, a 7 iron has 35 degrees of loft and so on. So your choice of the two wedges should be to complete your shortest irons in a manner that gives you the best opportunity to score—one option might be a sand wedge of 56 degrees for common chip/pitch shots and sand bunker play and a gap wedge of 50-52 degrees that fits neatly between your pitching wedge (usually 46-48 degrees) and the sand wedge providing a continuous, progression of lofts. In this option, you would basically continue a loft differential of four or maybe five degrees through this series of clubs.

A second option might be to increase the lofts in jumps of six to seven degree increments. In this scenario, your pitching wedge would be followed by a 54 degree sand wedge (possibly bent to 53 degrees) followed by the most lofted club in your set, a lob wedge of 60-62 degrees. A reputable dealer with a loft and lie adjustment machine will be able to add or reduce the loft of each wedge by a degree or two in order to optimize the spacing of lofts among the clubs at this end of your set. Most retailers, club -fitters or professionals will work with you to check the lofts of your clubs and refine your equipment to avoid excess gaps or uneven spacing of your wedges for a nominal fee. (In my own bag, my pitching wedge has a loft of 47 degrees, my sand wedge has 54 degrees of loft and I carry a 60 degree lob wedge.)

Again review your decision keeping in mind a gradual and progressive spacing of the lofts with the comfort and need you have to play shots from various distances and conditions based on the *home course(s)* you typically play. Players who consistently find themselves with short approach shots into par 4's and par 5's because of their ability to hit their driver and other long clubs great distances will be better served to carry three additional wedges after their pitching wedge. The typical set-up would be one that continues a tighter four degree spacing sequence—pitching wedge (47-48 degrees), gap wedge (52 degrees), sand wedge (56 degrees), and lob wedge (60 degrees). Of course, you might consider a slightly stronger lofted variation (47, 51, 54, 58) or a slightly weaker variation (48, 53, 58, 63) depending on your skill level, your comfort in using each club and the frequency that you would be called upon to use these clubs during a round. A proper configuration of wedges is a personal decision that you should develop in consultation with a PGA Professional who you trust with your game.

What is the proper amount of bounce for each of my wedges?

Every major club manufacturer prints brochures with product details or lists the information on its website regarding the various loft and bounce combinations available in their different wedge series. Bounce is a design feature of the sole of irons and wedges where the trail edge of the sole is lower than the leading edge. This keeps the club from excessively digging into the turf or sand during impact. A higher bounce will keep the club accelerating forward through impact rather than digging deeper and losing speed. An important part of learning how to successfully play shots from sand is developing an understanding of how to activate the bounce of the club during impact and mastering that technique which is unique feature of bunker play.

Study this information, determining which lofted wedge you will use to play most of your shots from greenside sand bunkers. That wedge should have at least eight degrees of bounce or preferably a little more, say 10-14 degrees. The rule of thumb is if the sand is softer and thicker use a wedge with more bounce and a wider sole. Conversely, if the sand if firmer and thinner use a wedge with less bounce and a thinner sole. The second or third wedge you select for your bag should have moderate bounce (six to ten degrees) unless you are trying for a specific variation or option.

An example would be my two wedges—54 degree sand wedge with 14 degrees of bounce and a 60 degree lob wedge with eight degrees of bounce. The leading edge of my lob wedge sits much tighter to the ground/surface. It will dig more in a descending manner if I'm not careful with my swing, but it also allows me to accelerate the clubhead into the ball without fear that the club's bounce will cause the sole to deflect off the surface resulting in a thin hit or skulled shot.

Like most things in life, wedge selection is a matter of personal preference. You should try to make a selection of loft and bounce options that give you the best tools for the most common jobs, knowing full well that you cannot possibly carry a specific club for every shot you encounter, especially at either end of your iron set.

Later, we will discuss the myriad of partial swings and touch shots we use our wedges for in the chapters of Part Two.

For your information, most touring professionals will be fit by their sponsoring club manufacturers for up to a dozen different wedges with a variety of lofts, bounces and sole widths. This affords them the flexibility to customize their wedges to the specific course conditions they encounter on a week to week basis. This might become necessary if a particular tour stop has experienced an exceptionally rainy weather pattern and the sand in the bunkers is firm and packed down. Most of us are better off simply creating a single, personal wedge set-up and then practicing and playing with those clubs for an extended period of time in order to develop the feel, judgment, techniques and skills for the shots we are required to play with our wedges during a round.

What are the keys to successful full swings with wedges?

There are two general swing keys: first of all, balance your static weight in your pre-swing set-up/stance with 60% of your weight on your lead leg and foot and 40% on your trail leg and foot; maintain that weight distribution and balance throughout the swing.

Secondly, maintain a connection between you upper arms and the sides of your chest or upper rib cage area during the swing. The power will be derived from the rotation of the upper torso (*your big or core muscles*) back and through the shot rather than the smaller muscles of the arms and hands. This technique increases consistency.

The stance and address position described above is one of the key elements of Palmer 60/40 Golf—balance 60% of your weight on the lead side (hip, leg and foot) and 40% on your trail foot. This slightly *right-centered* balance is different from the traditional 50%-50% weight distribution most of us have been taught in the past to create a proper stance.

Additionally, it is extremely important to maintain the majority of your weight on your right side throughout the swing, thus eliminating a side to side, or lateral swaying movement of your head, spine and upper body during the dynamic rotation of the swing. Keep your weight right-centered and the quality of your impact position will improve almost immediately.

Fundamentals

Grip: A neutral grip position with light grip pressure is best for full swing wedge play because you should hit these shots primarily by rotating the upper body back and through with soft, quiet arms and hands. The small muscles serve as the connection to the club and a neutral grip is recommended to make the club release and hand rotation smooth and natural. Other grip options related to the other swings will be discussed in future chapters.

Alignment: You should use a parallel right alignment system for all shots. The use of alignment sticks, rods or golf clubs on the ground while practicing is the most common way for golfers at every level to check their alignment for a shot. Place two sticks on the ground parallel to each other about 12 inches apart. The far stick is the ball aiming line and should be aimed directly at the flagstick or ball target. The closer stick should be aligned to a spot approximately five yards to the right of the ball target. Select an object slightly to the right of your ball target and point the closer stick directly at that aiming spot for your body lines (shoulders, hips, knees and feet), keeping both sticks parallel to each other and maintaining equal spacing between the sticks.

The ball should be placed just beyond the far stick so it is easy to align the leading edge of the club perpendicular to the stick without having any danger of hitting the stick during a swing. The closer stick is for parallel right body alignment. Your toes should be an equal distance from this stick setting up even alignment of your feet, knees, hips and shoulders on the same parallel right aiming line. These parts of your body create your *body lines* for proper alignment. The shorter the shot, the less space between the parallel right alignment and conversely, longer shots require more space between the body alignment spot and the ball target. So, if you have an 85 yard wedge shot and your ball target is the flagstick, your body lines should be aimed at a spot two or three yards parallel right of the flagstick (or ball target.) A driver swing aimed for the center of the fairway should have a parallel right body alignment spot ten to twelve yards to the right of the center of the fairway (or ball target.)

Parallel Right Alignment

Stance/set-up: Because your wedges are the shortest clubs in your bag, the wedge stance necessitates a deeper than usual knee bend to attain the proper height for the shot while maintaining proper spine tilt fundamentals. Also, because your wedges are short clubs, open your stance slightly by moving your lead foot about one inch back from the parallel right alignment position. This change in the position of your feet should also be matched by your hips and shoulders opening an inch to the right so that all of your body lines are parallel with each other.

Apart from those two differences, you should use the same fundamentally athletic stance/set-up for all of your clubs:

- chin up with approximately three inches between your chin and chest;
- straight or neutral spine and back (with shoulder blades pulled together to prevent a rounding of the upper back);
- bend at the hips to achieve a proper spine tilt of your upper body (approximately 25-35 degrees depending on the length of the club);
- arms hanging comfortably straight down from the shoulders;
- your weight center-balanced 60%-40% on the lead side;
- your weight in the center of each foot under the laces of the shoe, and
- maintain this proper posture during the dynamic portions of the golf swing—it promotes correct swing repetition and balance.

Footwork: The importance of *footwork* in golf is underemphasized and most often neglected as an instructional point in lessons. It is so important that I have included it as a separate fundamental in each of the five swings. With wedges, you should have the least amount of foot movement that you will have in any swing. In other words, your feet should basically stay flat on the ground until the follow through or the very end of the swing. Even at that point, your weight should be balanced at 70%-80% onto your lead leg and foot for a wedge swing (not much considering your starting position of 60% on the lead side) causing your trail heel to lift only slightly off the ground to help you maintain overall balance as you rotate to the target and onto your lead leg. In your initial set-up position, press the instep of the lead foot into the turf to establish a strong, solid connection with the ground and maintain that pressure during the swing.

Also, there should not be any rolling of the feet to either the outside or inside edges of your shoes during a wedge swing. If you cannot swing this softly or this much under control and achieve the required distance of the shot, switch to your next stronger lofted club so you can reach your desired yardage while still maintaining the quiet footwork that is ideal for controlling your wedge shots with optimal accuracy.

Backswing: Start the clubhead back low to the ground and by turning the shoulders in the initial phase of your torso rotation. Maintain a straight right arm and a soft left arm with the same "*Y*" of the arms and club going back as you established in your set-up position. By the time your hands are half-way into the backswing, your wrists should achieve a full *90 degree set or cocked* position. This should feel like the club is pointing up or that you are standing the club up at this point of the backswing. Turn your shoulders and chest while holding a straight right arm position and keeping the left elbow in close proximity of the left side of the rib cage as far as is needed to return the club to the ball with the required speed and force for your desired yardage.

You will frequently encounter distances other than the maximum yardage for a full wedge and will have to utilize one of the techniques that will be described in the chapter on hitting partial shots.

The type of swing you will use with wedges is basically a big muscle, core rotation back and through the ball with connected, quiet arms and hands. A simple one plane swing should be used as much as possible, again because accuracy is your chief goal. Generally, the issue of plane, either too steep/upright or too flat and around the body, is not too critical with wedges because the clubs are so short.

If you keep your upper arms connected to the sides of your rib cage and rotate the entire chest back and through impact, the club's plane will travel naturally and find a correct path on its own in both the backswing and forward swing.

Forward Swing: Before you start the club or any part of the body forward, it is imperative for you to complete, and I can't stress this enough, *fully* complete your backswing. A drill (Hold 2) will be described shortly that focuses on this concept and will help you form this good habit for every full swing club. Because your weight distribution is 60%-40% on your lead leg and foot, you should begin your forward swing with the single thought of rotating your lead hip back and away from the ball. Most golfers have been taught to begin the downswing from the ground up which promotes a slide forward toward the target with the knees and hips before the upper body starts to uncoil and rotate into the shot. This older notion creates a flaw in most swings and makes solid impact more difficult. The legs, core and arms fall slightly out of synchronization with each other and the proper body timing and club rotation becomes less likely at impact. One or two degrees of face angle change from the initial set-up position to the impact position will cause a significant loss of accuracy. This rhythm and body/arm connection should not be as difficult to maintain with wedges, but when you move to longer clubs and more forceful swings, the ideal sequencing, synchronization and timing will become more difficult to achieve and can produce much greater problems. This issue is the basis for developing a sound, repeatable golf swing.

Your eyes should be focused on a dimple or mark on the front half of the ball. The tighter the focal point your eyes send to your brain, the better the eye-hand coordination's response will be at the impact point of the swing. Wedges are designed and built purposefully with heavy swing weights, and because of this feature, forearm roll, hand rotation and club release will occur naturally and without any conscious effort. A wedge shot is almost always focused on accuracy—accuracy of both distance and line. In order to achieve this goal, you must make a controlled swing with very little movement. Maintaining your dynamic balance during and at the conclusion of a wedge swing is a must. When you have a chance, watch a professional tour event and focus on the simple and efficient swings golf professionals make when playing short wedge shots. Try to emulate and copy their timing, control, and balance during your swings.

Follow through: Complete the rotation of your hips, chest and shoulders toward your target. If you can hold your follow through position (belt buckle pointing at the target) while steadily maintaining your balance, you have made a correct swing with the proper amount of speed and force and achieved an athletic, coordinated movement with your body. Finishing all swings and holding the follow through position is an important balance drill (Finish and hold) that you should practice with all five swings.

Impact: Your goal should be to hit every shot in the center, or sweet spot of the club face. Force your eyes to concentrate on a specific spot (dimple or marking) on the ball during every swing, and make the necessary adjustments either slightly closer to the ball or further away from the ball until your contact point tightens to the center of the club face. In order to avoid thin or heavy (fat) impact positions, you must maintain the flex in your knee joints, especially the trail knee, which tends to straighten during the backswing because of inflexibility, strength issues, an excessively long backswing and/or the use of the 60%-40% right-centered balance concept. Impact is the best and most foolproof test to determine the quality of a swing. It is the point when all the techniques, concepts, variables and moving parts come together to produce a result. What occurs during the split second of impact determines the quality of the swing in general and is your starting point in analyzing the chain reaction of swing components that just occurred, both pro and con, and determining the appropriate on-course corrections that might be necessary before your next swing.

How/What to Practice

The first clubs you should always hit on the practice range should be your wedges. Start with short shots using your most lofted wedge and aim at a specific target; begin with short, 15-25 yard shots. Try to make solid contact and keep your body and head very still on these initial swings of the session. Gradually expand the length of your swings and aim at targets of progressively longer distances. The targets might be flagsticks, features on the range such as a mound, a bunker or simply a dark or light patch of grass. The important issue is to always aim at a specific target on every shot. Hit about a dozen balls with the most lofted wedge and then switch to your wedge with the second most loft.

Repeat the same warm-up strategy. Begin at longer distances, perhaps 60 yards, and quickly culminate about a dozen balls later at 85-95 yards or whatever the optimal distance is for your full swing with that club.

During your practice session, return every 10-15 minutes to these two wedges and hit a ball or two with each club again at a specific target—focusing on accuracy as well as distance control. Hit at least twice as many balls with your wedges as you do with your other clubs while on the range. You should have the goal of landing every shot within a five yard circle of each target. As you switch targets, also switch directions occasionally. This will force you to take a new stance and work through the entire aiming and alignment process as if you were playing on the course. This constant disruption of your routine is one of the unique challenges of playing golf and should be part of your work on the driving range.

At the conclusion of each practice session, hit three or four full swing wedge shots. The purpose of coming back to your wedges is that they are important scoring clubs that you will use many times in almost every round. You want to feel confident in your ability to hit accurate shots with these clubs when those situations arise. Also, it is a good idea while practicing to vary the lengths of the clubs and the different feel of each club you are using in that it simulates the challenge of constantly switching from one club to another and changing our stance/set-up, alignment fundamentals and targets as you experience going from one shot to another while playing a round of golf.

Drills for Wedges

One Arm Swings: Left arm—hit short shots of about 15-20 yards with the focus of keeping your body very still and attempting to hit

14

the ball solidly in the center of the club face. Try to feel the weight of the clubhead using a very light grip and letting the loft of the club add height to the shot with a *soft* trajectory. The left elbow is bent slightly as it would be for any swing and the left arm hangs down naturally in a relaxed position. It should feel like the weight of the clubhead gathers at the completion of the backswing and then falls forward by the natural force of gravity at the start of the forward swing rather than your hand pulling the club downward.

Right arm—repeat the procedure of the previous drill. However, you will notice with this arm (the lead and non-dominant hand) the ball will have a lower, more boring trajectory. Again, the important points of this variation of the drill are to maintain a very still body and head while rotating the chest and shoulders in order to swing the club and to hit the ball solidly on the center of the club face, this time with a straight right arm; the right elbow joint *firm and locked*. Think of honing your eye/hand coordination during this drill. Focus on solid ball contact and eliminate unnecessary body movement while practicing. Your short shots will become much easier when you play them with both arms. Hit ten shots for each variation.

Flat Feet Drill: Make 3/4 speed swings with your weight balanced 60%-40% in a right-centered manner keeping both feet flat on the ground throughout the swing. The heels stay grounded and try to maintain flat feet without allowing your weight to *roll* to the inside and outside edges of your shoes during these practice shots. Start with an effort level of a 50% swing and gradually increase your acceleration until you can no longer keep your feet flat during the swing. Practicing shots hit with slower swings over time will have a profound benefit to your overall balance, control and ball striking. Hit ten shots to a comfortable distance between 50-75 yards depending on the club.

Hold 2 Drill: Take your stance setting-up at a specific target that requires a *full swing* with your sand wedge and work through your total list of fundamentals for the wedge swing. Complete the backswing and *FREEZE!* Hold that position for a full two count with absolutely no movement forward or downward. Then begin the down swing by rotating the lead hip away from the ball. Allow the big muscles of the upper body to follow the rotation naturally into impact. Once you get the timing of this drill perfected, you will be amazed that the ball will fly practically the same distance as it would using a continuous swing. The drill demonstrates the importance of the two separate components or directions of every swing, and it provides evidence that if both parts are completed properly, even with a full two second hesitation at the transition point, the correctness of your fundamentals will improve your timing and balance creating effortless power through efficient energy transfer. Beginning the downswing with the rotation of the lead hip starts the core muscles turning from the hips up to the shoulders and activates the lower body in the proper sequencing that allows the arms to follow and produce effortless power and accuracy in the swing.

Hit 12-15 shots total—use the Hold 2 technique for two shots, then take a regular, continuous swing with a smooth, unhurried transition point.

Repeat the drill five times.

Checklist/Video: After you have warmed-up, have a friend, family member or your PGA professional take some photos or a few videos of you hitting wedges. Review the images with an eye on the following points:

- right-centered weight balance 60%-40% maintained from set-up through the swings;
- deeper knee flex appropriate for wedges;
- trail knee maintains a flexed position during the swings;
- upper arms stay connected to the sides of the rib cage throughout;
- rotate chest and shoulder back and through as the engine of the swings;
- head should stay level and with little or no movement during the swings;
- maintain a straight right arm and a full wrist set of 90 degrees;
- carefully maintain the same spine angle or tilt during both parts of the swing; and

16

- check that your divots occurred after impact and in front of the ball.

Fitness/Exercise: *Always consult with your doctor before starting any exercise program. The fitness/exercise suggestions in this book should be used only by golfers in good health. Use common sense, adapt the suggestions to fit your current health concerns, or skip these sections if appropriate. Stop immediately if you experience any pain or discomfort and check with your physician.*

Trunk rotations: Hold a medicine ball, dumb bell, or weight plate in front of you and close to your stomach. Bend your knees slightly and slowly rotate your chest and upper body to the left and to the right while keeping your belt buckle facing forward and maintaining your knee flex. Gradually extend your arms as you continue your rotations until eventually your arms are fully extended. Maintain the connection between your upper arms and your chest throughout.

Continue rotations and slowly return your arms and the weighted object back to your stomach. A second variation is for the same rotations as described above but this time allowing your hips to also rotate with the core muscles. Each hip should rotate backwards, not from side to side. The benefits of trunk rotations include strengthening of the core muscles, increasing flexibility in the lower back and hips and training the hips to move instinctively in the proper manner during your golf swings. Perform 20 rotations with each variation.

Squats: Using the same weight as in the trunk rotations, perform simple squats (as if you are sitting down on an imaginary chair) keeping your back straight, maintaining your overall balance and holding the weight close to your stomach. As you feel comfortable, deepen the squat slightly. The benefits of squats include strengthening your upper leg muscles and hips which are important stabilizers in the golf swing and help us retain leg flex, increase speed and maintain our dynamic balance during full swings. Perform 20 squats per day.

Chapter 2 Irons

Simply stated, irons continue the role of wedges—hitting approach shots into greens with both directional accuracy and proper distance. In spite of advances in club design and improvements in the forgiveness of off-center hits, iron shots still require the highest degree of precision.

Also, in order to hit a proper iron shot, the bottom of your swing arc must occur after impact with the ball and in front of the original ball position. This *bottoming-out* of the swing's arc after impact creates a divot in front of the ball. Therefore we will spend the majority of our time in this chapter working through the particular elements and unique techniques related to making effective iron swings that are specific to these clubs.

Key Points for Irons: Q & A

How many irons should I carry?

In recent years, club manufacturers have made significant improvements in utility/rescue/hybrid clubs, thus making long irons virtually obsolete. One irons, two irons and in most cases, three irons are not even included in new sets of irons and are only available, if available at all, by special order. Long irons were always the most difficult clubs to hit consistently well, so the advent of hybrid club technology made the decision easy for most golfers, including professionals who play the game for a living.

Unless you are a highly accomplished player, your first, or longest, iron probably should be a four iron, and in some cases, a five iron. At the other end of your set of irons, you will need to decide whether the last club will be a nine iron or a pitching wedge.

I prefer completing the set with the pitching wedge, but a trend that has become popular with many players is to match the pitching wedge to the gap, sand and/or lob wedges. If you decide to stop your matched irons at the nine iron, most manufactures will honor the request at no additional cost, but usually through the custom or special order process. Regardless, the ending point of this question is that you should carry fewer irons (for example 4-PW, 5-PW, or 4-9) than you did as little as ten years ago when virtually all iron sets were built and sold in sets of nine clubs (2-PW) or eight clubs (3-PW).

Should I play with forged or investment cast irons?

Again, golf club manufacturers have made tremendous progress in the production processes and materials used to construct both types of irons. Also, these same advancements have made it possible to manufacture irons that are comprised of multiple metals and plastic materials and designed with a variety of cavity shapes. Cast clubs feel as good if not better in some cases than forged irons and are generally more forgiving. A decade or two ago, forged irons were all muscle back blades and investment cast materials were the only way to produce cavity back irons. The differences between the two styles has been shrunk considerably and the styles merged because of advances in design, compounding and head manufacturing by specialized companies that produce iron heads. In some ways, the type of metal used in making the club is more important than the manufacturing process.

You should play whichever irons best fit your age and skill level, and you should play the irons that provide you with the most confidence when you are getting ready to play a shot. There are many, many touring professionals who play investment cast or multi-material manufactured irons. Conversely, most amateurs can play forged irons more effectively than they might otherwise believe because of today's built-in forgiveness and larger sweet spot designs.

Should I be custom fit for my irons?

Absolutely! Research conducted by club manufacturers over many years indicates that a very high percentage of players do not need shorter or longer clubs, but an authorized club fitter or PGA professional can easily determine if you fall into the small percentage of people who, in fact, would benefit from non-standard length clubs. Most golfers can be properly fit with standard clubs because taller players generally have longer arms and shorter players generally have shorter arms, so length usually becomes a moot point.

Attend a *Demo Day* at a sponsoring facility and discuss this question with a club representative or PGA professional if you are curious about the issue of club length.

More importantly, however, is the question of *lie-angle* when it comes to custom fit irons. For one thing, the major club manufacturers use slightly different standards for their iron sets, and your physical characteristics (height, stance, arm length and swing mechanics) can have a significant bearing on the lie-angle that is correct for you. Over time, players adjust to their equipment. However, it is important for you to verify with a professional that your irons are fitted with the proper lie-angle for your body and swing characteristics, that the clubs maximize your ability to return the clubhead to the ball squarely and that the lie angle does not impede the accuracy of the shot.

What are the keys to hitting consistent iron shots?

The single most important rule to hitting good iron shot is to use the 60%-40% right-centered weight and balance distribution for your final stance/set-up position. 60% of your static weight should be on the lead leg and foot. This concept is essential with iron swings. This right-centered position effectively relocates the ball position back about an inch because your spine has moved that much to the right. In order to compensate for that inadvertent change in ball position, you should alter your actual ball position a corresponding inch forward to a central point between your two feet; as you would position the ball if you were using a 50%-50% stance. Your hands should be pressed forward, slightly ahead of the ball (about an inch) even after this adjustment.

The second most important point in hitting solid irons shots is to maintain a consistent spine angle tilt from the start to the finish of the swing. Players lacking flexibility or over-swinging during the backswing will oftentimes raise-up and lose their starting spine angle, usually straightening the trail leg. A loss of the flex in the trail knee joint can also cause the trail hip to change positions and push/slide the spine into a lateral movement. Once this happens in the first half of a swing you are forced to recover to your original stance during the second half of the swing. The timing and return into the initial set up position is difficult to do on a consistent basis—for this reason, you are better off developing a backswing that doesn't create unnecessary movements or positions from which you have to recover in order to hit the ball properly.

Try to stay low and level maintaining your initial stance/set-up position in order to compress the ball into the ground and then take a small divot. Your arms will naturally elongate because of the centrifugal force generated during your forward swing, so all of the concepts we want to happen at the point of impact should occur naturally as long as your upper body doesn't raise-up during the swing. The finer points of this key will be discussed in greater detail later in the chapter.

Fundamentals

Grip: A slightly stronger grip is necessary for effective iron play. Players should link their hands together incorporating either the interlocking or overlapping system, so the hands work in unison.

The right hand should move over more to the left on the grip so you can see two or three of the knuckles at the base of your fingers (at least the index and middle finger knuckles). The left hand should match the right hand in a slightly strong position on the grip of the club. A stronger grip for iron play is important because of the club's significant interaction with the turf through the impact zone when it hits the divot. You want your hands to be firing or turning over with force in order to square the club face properly and to withstand the digging of the iron into the ground.

Alignment: Parallel right alignment is a critical concept to utilize during iron play. From 100 yards, set-up your body's alignment lines to a spot approximately three yards right of the ball target; from 200 yards, your body should be aligned to a spot approximately six to eight yards right of the ball target. A key is to avoid aiming your feet, knees, hips and shoulders directly at the ball target. Be careful not to make this change unconsciously while you are making small, final adjustment steps just prior to starting the club in the backswing. Your feet, knees, hips and shoulders should all be square to one another and all of these *lines* should be aimed at a spot right of the ball target. Unfortunately, it is easy to set your feet on one line and as you take your final glace at the target, shift your hips and/or shoulders on a different line. Your club face is the only thing that is ever aimed directly at the ball target.

The *lines* formed by your feet, knees, hips and shoulders are one of the starting points to check if you find yourself struggling with the accuracy of your iron shots.

Stance/Set-up: Take an athletic stance similar to that of a ready position used by players in other sports—baseball, football, volleyball, hockey and basketball. The stance is somewhat universal—knees flexed, bent over or tilted forward from the hips, with your back straight and your weight balanced under your shoe laces; not too far forward toward your toes and not too far back on your heels. Once you have this position, simply shift your overall static weight slightly to the lead leg and foot at a balance ratio of 60% on the lead side and then hold that set-up.

60/40 Right-centered balance

Your arms hang comfortably down under your shoulders—not too close to your body and not too far stretched out away from your mid-section (ideally six to eight inches from your belt buckle depending on the length of the iron; shorter clubs closer and longer clubs further).

Your spine should be relatively straight or neutral without much arch or bulge in the lower back and without *roundedness* in the upper back and shoulders—squeeze your shoulder blades together to inhibit this posture. Avoid dipping your head down to look at the ball; rather maintain three to four inches between your chin and your upper chest and tilt your eyes to see the ball, not your head. Keep your hips level in your stance; an easy way is to think of your belt or waist band being level, not tilted. Your trail hip might need to be lowered to achieve this position. All of these elements of correct posture are vitally important in order to give you the best chance of maintaining your dynamic balance and retaining your spine angle and alignment lines during the swing. Improper stance/set-up fundamentals create breakdowns in every swing.

Footwork: One of the most important elements in hitting solid iron shots is maintaining a right-centered position of stability that you rotate around in the swing. You will feel your weight shifting to different parts of your feet inside your shoes, but try to keep it centered as much as possible under your laces, avoiding a *rolling* to the inner or outer edges of your shoes, especially during the backswing. Flat footwork in your backswing is the best way to hold your angles and head position as still, or quiet as possible. Connect the instep of your lead foot firmly to turf to establish proper footing during the swing. The fewer the moving parts the better on iron swings. During your forward swing and following impact, allow your feet to move naturally to accept your body weight moving onto your lead leg. This also helps you maintain your overall balance and complete an effective follow through. Usually 95% or your weight will finish on the lead side at the end of a full iron swing, and your trail foot will be touching the ground only through the toe of your trail foot shoe.

Backswing: Start the club in motion away from the ball on a low, straight line for approximately 12 inches. Use a one-piece takeaway meaning the club and arms move with the shoulders as they start to rotate. As the clubhead naturally elevates from the turf, allow the toe of the iron to roll upwards toward the sky by gradually rotating your forearms and hands during the first three feet of the backswing. When your arms reach waist height, the toe of the club should be pointed straight up—check this position by swinging only that far and looking back at the clubhead's position. From this point, stand the club in a vertical position by setting or cocking your wrists and then continue your upper body rotation. Your natural swing plane will be achieved if you keep the connection between your upper arms and your chest intact.

This is the feeling many tour professionals are trying to memorize when you see them hold a glove or head cover under their arms while practicing or when they tuck some of their shirt sleeve into that area to hold during their backswing while playing.

This modern concept is of paramount importance because the connection helps to maintain the synchronicity between the big muscles of the core with the small muscles of the arms and hands during the swing. A full wrist set, or cocked position, should be established somewhat early during the backswing, culminating in a 90 degree angle at the top of the backswing. The club shaft should be as close to parallel with the ground at that final position.

Proper wrist set at the completion of the backswing

Also, it is very important to keep your knees flexed during your swing in the same angle that you established during your pre-swing stance. The right arm should stay fully extended and straight with your hands far away from your face. Finally, your eyes should focus on a dimple or mark near the front half of the top of the ball and try to maintain that point of vision on the spot through impact.

Forward swing: The first move of your body that starts the club from the zero point of transition into the forward swing should be the lead hip moving back away from the ball. Think of your hips rotating 15-25 degrees on the backswing, significantly less than your shoulders rotate, and 45-90 degrees during the forward swing—with the emphasis on the hips *rotating* rather than *sliding*. At the top of your backswing, your trail hip should have rotated back away from the ball a few inches and the opposite action with your lead hip is the initial move that starts the chain reaction of the other body parts in the forward swing. The uncoiling of the upper body's core muscles in the reverse rotation of this part of the swing will trigger the gathering of speed of the arms, hands and club into impact.

Maintain a straight right arm with a firm elbow joint for speed and consistent length into the bottom of the swing arc, and maintain your wrist-set or cocked position as long as possible until it naturally unhinges and rotates on its own very late in the forward swing close to impact. If these elements are in tandem with the body's weight shift from 60%-40% to 95%/5% onto the lead side, the club will be moving with optimal speed and force at impact. Then, your eye-hand coordination and hours of repetition through practice hopefully will cause the ball to be struck near the center of the club face, transferring the maximum energy into the shot.

Follow through: Attempt to finish all iron swings in balance and with your weight fully transferred onto your lead side, but equally important, you should rotate your hips and chest fully facing your ball target at the conclusion of the swing. Players should make iron swings with approximately 85% of their maximum swing speed and force. Oftentimes, this suggests selecting one stronger lofted club than the yardage suggests and making a smooth swing with even tempo. It will be much easier to stay on balance if you do not swing at your maximum speed. Also, an overall reduced swing speed will increase the frequency of solid shots struck in a tighter pattern in the center of the club face. A ball receives the optimal energy transfer from the sweet spot of the club face and will usually fly the proper yardage. This is a primary goal in iron play. Shots that fall short of the desired yardage were almost always not struck with the center of the club face. Model your iron swings after those of many LPGA touring professionals—their rhythm, balance and fundamentals are often flawless examples of efficient, effective swings.

Impact: As previously discussed, there is very little margin for error in hitting proper iron shots and impact immediately reveals everything about the quality of a particular swing. Keep your head steady with your eyes tightly focused on a dimple or mark on the ball through impact and until the ball disappears. Ideally, hit the ball first and then take a small divot in front of your ball's position. An easy way to remember this proper sequence is to remember the phrase, *ball-turf,* which describes correct impact.

Proper "ball, then turf" iron impact

Your divots can reveal a great deal about your swing—for the most part, your divot should be straight on the ball target line. If the divot is angled too far to the left or right of the ball target line, it reveals the club path was exaggerated on an incorrect line. A necessary correction should be readily apparent to you, so rehearse the corrected proper path before you return your club to your bag.

A divot that is too deep, or no divot at all, also provides you with immediate feedback and a clear indicator of a swing error. Too deep of a divot suggests too steep of a plane or descending path of the club into the ball. The cause might be too upright of a stance, too vertical of a swing plane, standing too close to the ball in your set-up, ball position too far back in the stance or not enough upper body rotation in the swing— all of which could have caused too much downward drive and a loss of spine angle and a dipping lateral slide into the impact zone of the shot. On the other hand, a loss in knee flex or a change in spine angle tilt might be the causes for the club entering the contact zone on an elevated path and causing a thin strike too high on the ball.

Pinching or compressing the ball into the turf on iron shots is very important because it creates spin on the ball. Spin is necessary to control an iron shot. Compressing the ball into the turf and creating spin translates into distance control, both the distance and direction the ball flies in the air and the amount of *roll-out* the ball has once it lands on the ground. Try to hit every iron shot flush on the center of the club face. Focusing on a dimple will help with your eye-hand coordination and make adjustments from swing to swing in an attempt to find of the sweet spot of the club face as often as possible.

Nothing in golf feels as good as a perfectly struck iron shot. The effortless power you feel when maximum energy transfer occurs and the resulting unwavering pin-point trajectory/flight of the ball toward the target makes for one of the most satisfying experiences in all of sports.

How/What to Practice

When you go out to the practice range to hit balls, start with your shortest irons and move progressively through the set finishing with your longest iron. Limit your ball count to six to eight balls per club.

Every shot should be aimed at a specific target, preferably a flagstick. Your key thoughts for practicing iron swings include the following items:

- make solid contact;
- limit yourself to swing with no more than 85% of your maximum speed and force;
- 60%-40% right-centered weight balance ratio in your stance and swing;
- upper arms connected to the sides of the rib cage;
- straight right arm with solid/tight elbow joint;
- complete the turn/rotation of the upper body in the backswing;
- start the forward swing with the lead hip moving back and away from the ball;
- maintain your initial spine angle/tilt throughout the swing; and
- finish the follow through with a complete rotation of the upper body (chest and belt buckle) toward the target.

Focus on one key at a time, but as you practice switch your thought from one element to another. During the pre-swing phase of a golf swing, your mind can review several items on your checklist but once the club is in motion, limit your mind to only *one swing thought* or concept. Toward the end of your practice session it is helpful to alternate shots with clubs of different lengths. This forces you to make the necessary adjustments in your stance/set-up, alignment and ball position as you are forced to do while playing golf.

Drills for Iron Swings

One foot back: Take your complete stance in preparation of hitting a shot. Pull your trail foot straight back approximately 12 inches and balance that foot on your toes. Almost all of your static weight now will have shifted to your lead leg and foot. Take a few slow practice swings to get accustomed to this feeling of exaggerated imbalance. Begin to hit balls with progressively short and slow swings and gradually work your way up to moderately fast, full swings.

Stance for One Foot Back Drill

Maintain your dynamic balance throughout these swings with the goals of hitting the ball with the center of the club face and striking the ball first and the ground second. Incorporate as many of your swing keys that you can as you grasp the feeling of the exaggerated right-centered balance position as a key iron play fundamental. Hit 10-15 shots; return to your normal 60%-40% right-centered balance for three to five shots; repeat the drill with the trail foot dropped back for three to five shots and complete the drill with one

30

more 60%-40% cycle. It's a good idea to do this drill during the early part of your iron practice—maybe 1/3 of the way through your overall practice session.

L Drill: This drill promotes solid contact, rapid hand rotation, and a full club release through the impact zone. Start with your hands at waist level in the backswing position and the club at a 90 degree angle to the ground, or pointing straight up to the sky with your hands in a fully cocked position. The arms and club should look like the letter L. Your stance is normal with the 60%-40% right-centered weight balance. Your upper arms are connected to the sides of your chest as if you were holding a glove under each arm in the arm pit area. Maintain a stiff, straight right arm and begin the forward swing by rotating the lead hip away from the ball and allowing your chest to rotate from the loaded backswing position through impact and into the finished rotation position on your lead side. Your hands will fire or turn-over at impact in much the same way as a short whip action. Both arms should be straight and fully extended past impact and the right elbow stays firm and locked until deep into the follow through when the arms relax and fold naturally near your right shoulder.

If you do the drill correctly, the lead hip will rotate back away from the ball about three or four inches and your arms and hands should follow the rotation of your chest to the right following impact, not straight down the ball target line. The hand action learned during this drill will train the muscles to instinctively release the club properly through the impact zone. Hit eight to ten shots with a 6 or 7 iron, and then hit three shots with your regular full swing feeling the increased speed caused by the proper release of the club through impact. Repeat the sequence several times switching clubs occasionally. This drill can be done at any time during the iron portion of your practice session.

Checklist/Video: The following items are the key concepts that you should monitor for effective iron swings:

- weight balanced 60%-40% on the lead side during the swing and finishing with at least 90% of your weight on the lead leg at the follow through position;

- slightly stronger grip;
- straight right arm;
- *quiet* footwork—mostly solid, flat feet with weight centered under your shoe laces;
- strike the ball first and the turf second taking a small divot;
- try to hit the ball in the center of the club face;
- maintain your upper arm connection to both sides of your chest;
- power and control comes from the rotation of the core (big) muscles—your arms and hands should feel as though they are along for the ride;
- finish your backswing completely before any movement into the forward swing;
- after a split-second pause at the conclusion of the backswing (transition) begin the rotation of the forward swing slowly and smoothly with the lead hip moving away from the ball, not sliding forward toward the ball target;
- gradually build the speed of the swing into the impact zone where the club is moving at the greatest speed; and
- completely rotate your upper body toward the target to complete the follow through—eyes, chest and belt buckle facing the ball target—and hold the finish position or trophy pose with proper balance.

Ask a friend or family member to take pictures or video with a cell phone or digital camera while you are hitting iron shots—there are six key areas to review in the images:

1. check the position of your arms and club about one foot into the backswing—look for the early chest rotation with connected upper arms and the club relatively low to the ground and beginning to rotate;

2. look at an image when your hands are at the height of your waist in the backswing—in these photos look for a straight right arm, a continuation of the chest rotation with the arm connection and the wrists set at 90 degrees and the club shaft pointing up to the sky;

3. at the top of the backswing check for the following—club shaft parallel to the ground, shoulders rotated with the lead shoulder pointing down at the ball, straight right arm, flex in the trail knee joint, 60% of your weight center-balanced slightly on the lead side, feet flat on the ground, and your head in roughly the same position as it was at the beginning of the swing—not higher or lower and no further left or right;

4. immediately after the transition pause and at the beginning of the forward swing—check your lead hip position to verify a movement away from the ball is backwards and without a forward right slide; look at your wrist and club angles to see if you have maintained your wrist set (holding the lag position of the club) without unhinging the wrists;

5. in the impact zone check your impact position—your arms should be fully extended and your weight should be braced against a straight right side while your upper body and hips are rotating to the right without a forward slide; ball contact should be first and contact with the turf, or divot, should follow the strike and your eyes should be focused on the ball; and

6. in your follow through—check to see if you maintained your dynamic balance with a less than maximum swing speed and if you held your finish position for a few seconds at the end of the swing.

Fitness/Exercises * Always consult with your doctor before starting any exercise program. The fitness/exercise suggestions in this book should be used only by golfers in good health. Use common sense, adapt the suggestions to fit your current health concerns, or skip these sections if appropriate. Stop immediately if you experience any pain or discomfort and check with your physician.*

Hammer curls: With a dumbbell or a heavy hammer—hold the object straight up and down with your arm waist high and in front of you; move the top of the object toward you and then move it forward away from you hinging and unhinging the wrist joint in much the same way as you would when using the hammer to hit a nail. This exercise will strengthen and improve flexibility in your wrist joint.

This position in the golf swing is the wrist set at the top of the backswing. Do a few repetitions of sets of ten wrist sets with each hand.

Wrist curls: Dumbbell—sitting in a chair, lay your forearm on your upper leg so only your wrist and hand extend beyond your knee holding the dumbbell with your palm up. This should isolate the lift to the curling of the wrist joint. Curl the dumbbell 25 times and then turn the hand over so your palm is facing the ground and repeat 25 curls. Do two sets with each variation and with both hands, wrists and forearms.

Core exercises: Lie on the floor on your back—perform stomach crunches in any style that is comfortable for you (research different variations online or check with your doctor). Secondly, with your back on the floor, bring your knees up and place your feet flat on the floor. Gently allow your knees to fall to the right and then hold for five seconds; return to the starting position and then allow your knees to fall to the left and hold for five seconds. Thirdly, with your back flat on the floor, lift your knees and feet off the floor and peddle a bicycle for 20 seconds with your legs in the air. Finally, in a push-up position but with your elbows on the floor and your hands together, lift your entire body about ten inches off the floor balancing only on your toes, elbows, forearms and hands in a plank position—hold for ten seconds. Repeat the core exercises several times.

Standing exercises: Toe touches; raise your arms above your head and take at least five full seconds to move your hands toward your toes as far as you can comfortably reach; hold that position for a full five seconds and then take a full five seconds to slowly return to your initial standing position. Repeat three times.

Punch rotations: Standing with your knees slightly flexed, perform tight trunk rotations alternating from left to right with simulated boxer upper-cut punches across and in front of your body. Gradually extend your arms from bent at the elbows to fully extended (simulating jab punches) and then back to bent for approximately 20 rotations.

Karate Kid one foot poses: Stand on one foot for ten seconds; lift both arms at your side at shoulder height. Lift the knee of the raised leg so your foot is about ten inches off the ground. Maintain your balance and slowly rotate your upper body to the right and return and then to the left and return. Switch to the other foot and repeat the exercise. You should feel many small muscles in the leg and ankle *firing* to help stabilize your balance. Repeat several times.

Chapter 3 Hybrids and Fairway Metals

One of the biggest advances in golf equipment during the past 15 years has been in the evolution of hybrid clubs. These transition clubs have virtually made long irons obsolete, and with good reason.

Golf courses are longer and demand longer approach shots. Hybrid clubs offer a distinct advantage over long irons in that they produce a longer and higher ball flight trajectory with more backspin which results in the ball landing softly from a steeper angle and with less roll-out.

The combination of longer shafts, greater clubhead mass, wider soles and exceptional forgiveness make hybrids immensely easier to hit consistently than long irons. They provide a unique blend of distance and accuracy and help players of all ability levels have more success with long approach shots to par 4s and par 5s.

Perhaps the hybrid's greatest asset, however, is the ability to advance the ball significant distances from the rough. These clubs are easy to use and make the transition between your irons and your fairway metals seamless and effortless.

The change of materials from wood to metal in fairway metals clubs has also made these clubs much more forgiving and thus easier for all golfers to use with greater proficiency. The effective sweet spot and the surrounding area that still transfers great energy into the ball is the result of advances in the materials used to build the clubs and in the clubhead's designs. Longer graphite shafts, designed and weighted specifically to maximize the playability of hybrids and fairway metals have also played a large part in the advancements of these clubs.

Key Points for Hybrids and Fairway Metals: Q &A

Which types of these clubs and what lofts should I carry?

As with wedges, you will have many choices to consider when assembling this part of your bag. Start with one end or the other.

Ask yourself how many clubs you can carry in this section of your set and what distances you want to cover with full swings at these upper yardages based on your usual playing conditions and home/favorite courses. Also, consideration should be given to which of these types of clubs, hybrids or fairway metals, you prefer using (or feel better to you) and which of these types of clubs you have the most confidence hitting from a variety of situations on the course. The answer to this question could be your tipping point when making a decision about how many and which combination of these clubs you select for your bag, say two hybrids and one fairway metal or the reverse.

The lofts are self-explanatory, but remember that a 17 degree hybrid will fly a different yardage and with a different trajectory than will a 17 degree fairway metal. The lengths of the clubs and the shapes of the clubheads cause shots with each to be very different from one another. The single best way to experiment and work towards your decision regarding your clubs of choice is to devote a few hours of your time to actually trying different clubs at a comprehensive *Demo Day* in order to see the differences in ball flight, club speed, feel and distances from the vast array of choices. The host course and some of the club manufacturers might offer you discounts on any purchases made at one of these events. Also, these promotional events afford you the opportunity to try a variety of brands, shafts, flexes, clubhead designs (off-set or straight) and lofts of many different clubs in a short period of time.

Are different types of swings required to hit these two types of clubs?

Yes. Fairway metals are designed to be hit with a sweeping, shallow full swing with little or no divot—almost hitting the ball cleanly or picking the ball off of the turf, of course, depending on the lie. Hybrids, on the other hand, perform best when swung with a more descending or steeper angle into the impact zone, very similar to an iron swing. Ideally, you should take a small divot after contact, or at least, make contact with the turf following the strike. A key to hitting both fairway metals and hybrids is to complete a full backswing and to gradually generate clubhead speed in synchronization with your body rotation in the forward swing so that your greatest speed occurs just after impact. Because of the length of these clubs, you must keep the club accelerating into the follow through portion of the swing by continuing your upper body rotation to the target. Think of *swinging the club* rather than *hitting the ball*.

Fundamentals

Grip: Squaring the clubface at impact is extremely important with fairway metals and hybrids because the ball is traveling a long way.

The first goal should be to keep your ball flight within a tight dispersion range of your ball target; in other words, a shot that is hit off the target line should remain within ten yards on either side of that aiming point in order to avoid trouble or a high number on your scorecard. Therefore, begin with a neutral grip and make very small adjustments with your right hand only until you feel confident that you can control your shots with a consistent ball flight pattern (fade, draw or straight).

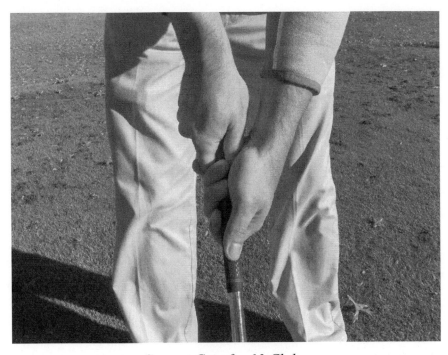

Correct Grip for 13 Clubs

Again, the goal should be to produce a repeatable swing with relatively high degree of accuracy toward your ball target. Pre-determining your desired shot shape is important with these longest clubs. If you can hit the ball straight, keep that as your main shot shape or trajectory, but also learn how to curve shots both left to right and right to left by making subtle changes to your grip, and if necessary your stance. Today's balls and clubs are designed to *minimize* spin, so it is easier than in the past to hit *straight* shots. Find a grip that produces a shot with little or no side spin and stick with it as your stock/routine grip.

Alignment: Align your body lines (feet, knees, hips and shoulders) at a spot approximately six to eight yards parallel right of your ball target. Try to find an object in the distance (a tree, a peak on a building, or a feature on the course such as a mound or an edge of a sand bunker) to use as the target marker to align your body lines.

Keep in mind that the ball target should rarely be directly at the flagstick. Rather, the ball target line will often be an opening leading onto the green or simply the center of the green, so your body should be aligned parallel right of *that* ball target and not the flagstick. Give yourself a healthy margin for error on such long shots. Hybrids and fairway metals have the primary function of distance with accuracy being an important, yet slightly secondary, objective.

Stance/Set-up: There are several key differences that must be noted when considering the stances you take with these clubs.

First of all, take a slightly wider stance with hybrids than you would for an iron swing just as you would for a progressively longer iron. As always, a 60%-40% right-centered balance ratio is recommended as the weight distribution for your final address position. With fairway metals take an even wider stance. Other than the driver, these are the longest clubs in your bag and you will make the longest and fastest swing with them. A wider stance will help stabilize your spine angle and maintain minimal head movement and lateral sway during such a dynamically charged and forceful swing.

Secondly, the ball position for these two clubs is farther forward toward your lead foot than with any other clubs except your driver. Hybrids should be played with the ball position one ball forward of dead center (the spot equally between your feet) and the ball position for fairway metals should be two or three balls forward of dead center.

Ball position for hybrid clubs and long irons

Again, an important reason for this difference is that hybrid swings should have a more descending arc into the impact zone, similar to iron swings, whereas swings with fairway metals should be more sweeping and on a shallower arc into the ball-contact area. Hybrid swings will often produce a small divot following the strike, and fairway metal swings will usually bottom-out with only a glancing interaction with the turf.

Use the same stance and set-up position for hybrid swings that you established for mid to long iron swings—slightly taller because of the club's length but with the same hip bend and spine angle that you use for iron swings, one that keeps your lateral movement minimal and centered directly over the ball during the swing. With fairway metal swings, your stance should have a tall, upright posture, with a smaller amount of knee flex and spine tilt than you have with your irons and wedges.

The taller and more upright stances for hybrids and fairway metals and the change in ball positions required to hit proper shots with these two clubs also creates a difference in the *shaft lean* associated with the final set-up positions. With hybrids, your hands should still be in front of the ball, but only slightly. So the shaft lean will be approximately five degrees to the lead side once you assume your final 60%-40% right-centered address position. The hand position for fairway metals should be directly in line with the ball or only the slightest bit ahead of the ball (a degree or two at most). As you look down, the shaft should look straight from above with virtually no forward lean or press—in other words the clubhead and shaft are in unison. One reason to pay close attention to shaft lean is a concern for *de-lofting* these clubs which have little loft to begin with and the effect that less loft will have on the ball's flight and trajectory. A second concern is the necessity of squaring the clubface at impact. If your hands get too far ahead of the ball during the forward swing, it is difficult to time the rotation of the club face to a square position, and it becomes easy to block shots directly to the left of your ball target or to flip the release of the club at impact, both caused by an initial faulty hand position.

Footwork: As we have already established, wider stances than usual are necessary for hybrid and fairway metal swings. Balance should be centered with a true 60%-40% ratio on the lead foot and leg for hybrid swings and only slightly less (a feeling of about 55%-45% on the lead side at the final address position) for fairway metal swings.

42

During the backswing, both feet should stay flat on the ground. You might feel a very small weight shift to your trail foot during a fairway metal swing. Try to keep that weight centered between your feet by pressing down the instep or inside edge of your trail shoe. In fact, angle your trail foot's weight and pressure onto the big toe and ball area of the foot, and brace that foot with the inside edge of your shoe to help establish a point of stability during the backswing.

Also, move your trail knee slightly toward the ball; this will also restrict lateral movement and create a solid base with the lower body in the backswing. This is especially important for these long clubs because the upper body rotation is very dynamic and a complete shoulder turn up to the transition point is necessary for a successful swing.

During the fairway metal forward swing, you might feel the trail foot pushing or driving the rotation of the hips and upper body. Again, because this is such a long swing, your trail foot should come off the ground earlier and more noticeably than you will feel it with hybrid or iron swings. Turn or open your lead foot shoe slightly toward the target (about five to ten degrees) in your final pre-swing stance so that it is in a better position to maintain your balance as your weight shifts with greater speed than with other swings to the lead side during and after impact.

Backswing: The backswing for hybrids is similar to your iron swings—a straight low push back of about 10-12 inches away from the ball starting with the chest's rotation and with your upper arms connected to the sides of your rib cage. A long, slow takeaway is best for fairway metals; the clubhead should stay low to the ground until it naturally lifts by the continuation of the upper body rotation.

By the time your hands reach waist height, the toe of the club should be pointed up to the sky and the wrist set should be 50%-80% completed.

Stand toe of club up in early backswing

Your right arm remains straight (elbow joint locked) through both the backswing and the forward swing. The extended right arm and club provides a constant length for the circle of the swing. Maintain a comfortable flex in your knees as you rotate the trail hip back several inches and the right shoulder rotates under your chin and *points* at the ball. Keep space between your chin and chest while your upper body completes its rotation around the spine. At the top of the backswing, your hands should be far away from your face by an extended right arm. The wrists are set at 90 degrees; the left elbow is bent and only a few inches from your chest. The club shaft is parallel to the ground, or as close as you can get it without going past parallel, and your back is pointed at the target when your backswing is completed at the transition point. Maintain your knee flex and keep your weight balanced on your lead side with the 60%-40% ratio.

Forward swing: The transition from the completed backswing and the beginning of the forward swing is of paramount importance with hybrids and fairway metals. A temptation is to try to hit the ball hard from the top of the forward swing usually with your dominant hand and arm (our dominant side subconsciously takes over) rather than actually allowing the lead side of our body to be the catalyst and controlling force for these swings. Rather than *hitting the ball with our hands*, think of *swinging the club with our body* using an even rhythm and tempo. The lengths of fairway metals and hybrids requires proper timing, synchronization and sequencing of the arms and core muscles to gather clubhead speed and to allow for proper shaft reaction in the impact area. This should all happen naturally with smooth rhythm. The lead hip should rotate backwards away from the ball to initiate the forward swing. Maintain the connection between your upper arms and chest during the swing. This connection usually eliminates concerns about the swing plane.

However, if your misses are curving away from the target because of excess spin, an improper plane could be the reason. You might have lost the connection between the arms and chest. One positive aspect of long shots is that a swing error is usually exaggerated because of the distance of the shot, so it is easier to identify the flaw in a particular swing and determine which correction(s) need to be made prior to the next swing with one of these clubs.

Follow Through: There is a large amount of centrifugal force that occurs during a hybrid and fairway metal swing, so your arms should naturally remain fully extended through the impact zone and into the initial part of your follow through. The clubhead will chase down the ball target line for a few feet after impact and then the arm and chest connection should pull the club to the right with the rotation of your hips and upper body. As your chest completes its rotation toward the target the arms will fold naturally near the right shoulder. As always, balance is a critical component to making effective swings with long clubs, and you will know immediately about the quality of the swing based on your ability to finish the swing on your lead side, belt buckle at the target, 90% or your weight on the lead leg and foot, and your trail foot only touching the turf with the toe of your shoe in order to maintain stability and balance.

Impact: Although hybrids and fairway metals are quite forgiving, off-center hits on the club face will result in a more dramatic loss of yardage than other clubs because of the relative correlation between the potential optimal distances of the clubs minus a percentage of energy loss because of inefficient impact. For example, a 200 yard hybrid shot minus 10% energy transfer = 180 total yards or a loss of 20 yards, whereby a 150 yard iron shot minus 10% energy transfer = 135 total yards or a loss of 15 yards.

A very important element in hitting solid shots with these long clubs is maintaining your height, spine angle and overall posture throughout the swing. Too often we drop the lead side of our bodies during the forward swing in an attempt to swing these clubs too fast and with too much force. Hybrid and fairway metal clubs are designed and constructed with plenty of power, as long as we gather gradual and continual clubhead acceleration and strike the ball as near as possible to the center of the club face. If your clubhead speed is moving at its fastest rate immediately following impact, your hands and arms will rotate and release the club properly squaring the club face correctly through the impact zone. Solid impact should be your first priority in making swings with hybrids and fairway metals. A well struck ball will fly the intended distance with the most accuracy, which is especially important on long shots.

How/What to Practice

The best way to practice making good hybrid and fairway metal swings is to hit shots with a full backswing, a smooth transition point, and with a forward swing of approximately 60-75 % of your maximum club speed. Initially, it will feel like you are swinging the club in slow motion. It will be difficult to keep your body in sync with your arms and the club. Your weight balance should be 60% right-centered and your stance should be more upright with less spine tilt than a typical iron stance. As you continue to warm-up your timing and eye-hand coordination, gradually increase the speed of your swings through a faster rotation of the upper body and a more active lower body. The club's speed will also increase, naturally. After 8-10 swings, you should be practicing full swings, under control, and without *hitting* the ball with your hands and arms. The core, big muscles should do the rotational work which initiates the *cracking of the whip* of your arms, hands and club through impact.

Practice your follow through with exaggeration to insure that you have turned your chest and hips fully toward your body alignment target.

Release the club with an effortless rotation of the wrists and hands and extend your arms down the target line before they follow your body to the right. As always, your grip pressure should be rather light to promote and not hinder a proper release through impact. Start your forward swing with a backward rotation of the lead hip away from the ball and maintain a straight right arm during the swing. Hold your final follow through position for at least three seconds, or until the ball hits the ground.

Drills for Hybrids and Fairway Metals

Feet together drill: Take a stance with the inside edges of your shoes only a few inches apart; your feet nearly are touching each other.

This is an anti-swaying drill, so feel the strong rotation of your upper body and hips around your spine without any lateral movement in the swing. Make several practice swings with a hybrid club at 50% of your normal swing speed in order to get accustomed to the balance of the drill. Now hit a few shots with the same 50% swings.

Slowly build up your swing speed until you are making full swings at 80% of your maximum speed and force. All of your other fundamentals stay in place, such as maintaining a slight knee flex and a straight right arm and rotating your chest and shoulders back and through the shots. Hit six to ten shots as the warm-up portion of the drill, and then hit three shots with your normal 60% right-centered stance followed by three shots again with your feet close together. Repeat the drill several times with your hybrid(s), and then perform the same drill with a fairway metal to practice the same concepts with the longer club.

1, 2, 3 drill: Many great players have practiced the rhythm and timing of their long club swings by using a pneumonic or counting routine. The easiest one is to mirror the full swing with the numbers 1, 2, and 3—1 being the backswing, 2 the top of the swing or transition point and 3 being the forward swing. The most important aspect of this drill is to create a speed in unison with the cadence of the counting of the numbers that is smooth and symmetrical and to connect your swing to that rhythm without rushing any one part of the sequence. Obviously 1, or the backswing, will be a relatively slow speed and 2, the completion of the full rotation of the backswing, is actually the transition point and the beginning of the movement forward. Number 3 will eventually become the fastest part of the swing through impact, so each of the three parts has a slightly different individual rhythm, but the main point to concentrate on is the overall pace the drill creates in your swing tempo; where each of the three parts of the swing is smooth and unhurried. Practice this drill with every hybrid and fairway metal.

Hit three shots with each club counting to yourself and linking your swing speed to the 1, 2 and 3 sequence. Then hit two shots without counting but attempting to replicate the same even rhythm during those swings. Repeat the drill with each club, counting for 3 swings, and then hitting two additional shots with the same tempo.

Complete two cycles of the drill with each or your hybrid and fairway metal clubs. If the counting example of 1, 2 and 3 is ineffective for your tempo, try another sequence such as "One And Two" or "Sev-en-teen." Matching your personal swing tempo to a cadence will produce the smoothness and evenness you are attempting to incorporate into your full golf swings over time.

Brush the grass: This is one of the oldest drills in golf and is still an effective way to practice rehearsing the *bottoming-out* of your swing arc at the ball.

Take a stance with the same fundamentals and earnestness you would if you were about to hit a ball, but for the drill focus on a specific spot on the turf or a clump of grass. Make a practice swing at 50% of your maximum swing speed attempting to brush the grass with the clubhead at the bottom of your swing arc through the impact zone. Repeat the drill gradually increasing the speed and intensity of your practice swing in 10% increments until you are finally swinging at 80% of your full swing speed. Then hit two shots reproducing the same swings you just made with the goal of hitting the ball solidly in the center of the club face.

Checklist/Video: A review of the fundamental concepts related to full swings with hybrid and fairway metal clubs includes the following items:

- taller posture and stance than with irons and wedges;
- a slightly wider stance;
- weight balanced at 60%-40% on the lead side with hybrids and a little more evenly balanced 55%-45% for fairway metals;
- hands in a more central position in front of your belt buckle with little forward shaft lean;
- ball position forward of center one inch for hybrids and three or more inches for fairway metals;
- straight right arm;
- maintain upper arms connection with the chest;
- totally complete your backswing before initiating the forward swing with the lead hip rotation away from the ball;
- hands high and away from the face at the top of the backswing and left elbow close to left ribs;
- smooth transition into the forward swing;
- retain tall posture and spine angle in forward swing without dipping into the lead side;
- gather clubhead speed gradually yet continuously on forward swing with peak acceleration occurring a few inches after impact;
- complete the rotation of the hips, chest and shoulders onto the lead leg and foot and fully facing the target; and
- hold your follow through position maintaining your balance with most of your weight on the lead side and your trail foot up on the toes.

Ask a friend or family member to either take a few video clips of you starting at your set-up position and finishing with your follow through or ask them to snap individual, discrete photos of you at six different points of your swing:

1. the starting address position;
2. hands waist high during the backswing;
3. the top of your backswing;
4. hands at waist height during the forward swing;
5. impact; and
6. the follow through position.

Compare your fundamentals to the ideal model discussed in this chapter. Focus on the checklist items and correct them one at a time during your practice sessions. Recheck your progress by having new photos or videos taken of your swings periodically. Doing this kind of work on the practice range is a good way to isolate separate elements of the swing, but, if possible, have a friend take videos or photos of you while you are actually playing holes on the golf course to verify the transference of your fundamentals into your swings within true playing conditions and competition. Ultimately, this is the best way to see if your swing improvements have become ingrained into your muscle-memory routine.

Fitness/Exercise *Always consult with your doctor before starting any exercise program. The fitness/exercise suggestions in this book should be used only by golfers in good health. Use common sense, adapt the suggestions to fit your current health concerns, or skip these sections if appropriate. Stop immediately if you experience any pain or discomfort and check with your physician.*

Windmill toe touches: (variation 1) Stand tall with your feet together and your arms fully extended in both directions so they are in a straight line with the top of your shoulders and you look like a *cross*. Now spread your feet about three feet apart. Touch your right hand past your left foot keeping your back tall and your legs straight.

Return to the upright starting position and then touch your left hand past your right foot; each time, return to the *cross* position, standing fully erect. Do 10-15 windmills relatively slowly to both sides.

(variation 2) Stand in the tall, cross position. Move your right foot about 24-30 inches forward in front of your body and left foot. You will now be tilted forward but maintain a straight spine, not bending at the hips. Try to achieve a spine angle that has a similar lean as if you were making a swing with a fairway metal. Rotate your hips, chest and arms in unison to the left and point your right hand at the ground and your left arm behind you; both arms are still fully extended at shoulder height. This should feel like the stretch you feel in your backswing. Hold this position for five seconds. Return to the starting position with a square chest pointing at the ground, and now rotate the upper body to right side extending the left hand at the ground in front of you and right hand behind you. This should feel like the stretch in the follow through position. Hold this position for five seconds, and then return to the starting position.

Repeat several times. Switch your foot position to the left foot forward and the right foot under your hips. Perform the same windmill extensions of this variation on this tilted plane. Repeat the entire exercise to both sides holding the stretch positions.

Hip and Leg Stretches: (variation 1) Stand about two feet from a wall or from a kitchen counter; place your hands flat on the wall or against the edge of the counter. Press your heels flat on the ground and hold the stretch in the backs of your legs for ten seconds. You should feel the deepest stretch in your legs below the knee in the calf and Achilles tendon/heel area.

(variation 2) Now drop your left leg back one or more foot behind your right foot and bend your left leg slightly at the knee joint. Press both heels flat on the ground and hold the stretch for ten seconds. Reverse your foot position and repeat the exercise. Stretch both sides several times.

(variation 3) Return to the position used in variation 2, with your left foot back and now rotate your left hip back and hold the stretch—keep your right knee slightly flexed and your right foot flat on the floor. Then return your hips to a square position and repeat three times. Reverse your stance by dropping your right foot behind the left foot. Rotate/pull the right hip back and hold, keeping a flex in the left knee and the left foot flat on the ground. Repeat this hip and hamstring stretch three times.

Arms and shoulders:

Push-ups: Do at least 25 per day. The goal is to work-up to full military style push-ups but if you need to adjust to a less stressful position in the beginning do so and use common sense as you increase the difficulty of the exercise over time.

Straight arm extensions: Weave your fingers together and then push them, palms up, over your head until your arms are fully extended and straight; hold for five seconds and then tilt your upper body five to ten inches to the left and hold. Press your palms up. Return your hands directly above your head in the starting stretch and then tilt your upper body five to ten inches to the right and hold. Repeat this exercise three times to each side. Make all stretching movements (both into and out of the stretch) slowly to maximize the gain in flexibility.

Shoulder extensions: Extend your arms behind your body (to your back side) and weave your fingers together. Straighten yours arms as fully as possible and lift your hands upward toward shoulder height. Pinch your shoulder blades together. You should feel a stretch in the front of your shoulders and chest. Relax the stretch by lowering your hands and then repeat the exercise three times, holding your stretch position for five seconds each time. This exercise stretches and *opens-up* the front part of your chest and shoulders. Our daily routines and work too often cause a rounding of the shoulders and a sunken chest. In golf it is very important to keep our chest area open (in a chest out and up military attention style) so we can make proper turns/upper body rotations, maintain our spine angle tilt and repeat athletic swings time after time.

Dumbbells: Develop a hand, wrist, arm, shoulder and back strengthening routine with a set of dumbbells that includes curls, rows, butterflies, and pulls in a variety of styles. Start with a comfortable weight and progress to heavier weights over time.

Many dumbbell routines and separate exercises are readily available online or in exercise books. For golf, your goals should be increasing strength and flexibility, not bulk.

Chapter 4 The Driver

Most golfers enjoy hitting their drivers more than any other club. But hitting your driver consistently with accuracy and distance is far more important to your score than the pleasure of crushing a drive.

In a typical round of golf, you will make between 10-14 driver swings, and as you know, the results of those shots set up your remaining shots on that hole in either a positive or negative fashion. If your drives finish in the fairway, it can make all the difference in how you score that day as well as increase your overall enjoyment of the round—that first shot on a hole dictates so many other things that follow.

Because the driver is usually the single most expensive club in your bag, club manufacturers spend a great deal of their research and development time and money competing for your loyalty. As a result, these clubs have never been better pieces of equipment. They are more forgiving and hit the ball farther and straighter than ever before in the history of golf. Today's drivers are so good that they are creating many problems for golf course owners related to the distances of holes, the costs of course designs and redesigns, and the associated expenses for water, fertilizer, seed and maintenance as holes and courses become longer.

Equally important, however, new drivers provide us with the opportunity to play better and more enjoyable golf on a regular basis.

The materials used in the manufacturing of drivers closely follow the leading edge of the metallurgical industry trends. Space age metals are fused together to create powerful and forgiving clubheads of such sizes that inspire greater confidence. Lighter, stronger and more consistent compositions of graphite materials have created a generation of shaft options that is staggering in both variety and quality. Moreover, adjustability options of weights, lofts and lie angles have allowed each golfer to further customize his/her own driver for superior feel and performance.

The driver swing, however, is quite unique compared to the four other swings of golf. To begin, the driver is the longest and usually the heaviest overall club in your bag. A ball struck with a driver is almost always elevated an inch or so off the ground on a tee which also has a significant effect on the design and shape of the driver.

The ball position for a driver is the furthest forward toward your lead foot and you are attempting to hit the longest shots during your round when you make a driver swing. Also, the clubhead of the driver is the furthest from your hands and eyes when you make contact with the ball and the clubhead is traveling over 25 feet during the swing and at faster speed than any other club you use.

These elements and others we will discuss make the driver one of the most exciting, challenging and rewarding clubs to swing.

Key Points for The Driver: Q & A

If drivers are so forgiving, why do I still lack accuracy and miss fairways?

The driver is your most powerful club and as a result, swing errors that impart unwanted backspin or sidespin to the ball are clearly and sometimes painfully exaggerated in the ball's flight. All of the elements that control trajectory are the most important reasons why you curve the ball with your driver— swing plane, angle of attack, club path and face rotation, squareness at impact and the synchronization and sequencing of your arms (small muscles) and your body (big muscles) are the five key variables to review when accuracy is a problem with this club. Also, your grip, your alignment lines and targets, as well as your stance and set-up fundamentals can have a significant effect on the results of these shots. Each of these concepts will be detailed in the remainder of this chapter.

How do I know which driver is the best one for me and how should I select the correct loft, shaft and setting for my driver?

Get help! The very best players in the world work with teaching professionals and club representatives to test the playing characteristics of their drivers to have them properly and personally fit to their golf swings and so should you. Very sophisticated equipment such as launch monitors can compare technical elements of club and ball speed, launch angle, carry distance and spin rate if you are the type of person who wants empirical data on how a driver is performing for you. Make an appointment with a recognized or certified club fitter in your area who you trust with equipment questions. Sometimes there is a nominal cost for these services, but the peace of mind and a better fitting driver are worth it. Also, the fee is often waived if and when you purchase a club from that retailer. This person should be reputable and respected in the area, not just a salesperson quoting numbers to you inside a retail store's netted hitting area. There are ways to make the numbers come out in favor of a particular club on this equipment, so always be wary and better yet, couple this data with your own visual ball flight observations when you have an opportunity to test the club outdoors. Many club manufacturers will bring their own technology and equipment to *Demo Days*, so these events provide an excellent opportunity to try out new drivers.

At an outside practice facility you should start by paying close attention to the feel and sound of a club. It usually takes only four to six shots to get acutely attuned to these club characteristics through your hands and ears, so be patient and take as much time as you need to determine if a particular club is worth testing further. As part of this data gathering process try as many drivers as you are interested in from the overall look of the product and the company reputation, and then narrow your test samples to no more than two or three drivers.

At most *Demo Days*, the representatives will gladly allow you to sample clubs on your own. If you are truly undecided about a club, hit four or five shots with a club and either rule it *in or out* as you keep experimenting. Advanced players start to subconsciously adjust to a club after only three swings, so limit your number of trial shots initially. Also, you should limit your total number of swings at a *Demo Day* to 60-85 swings. Any more swings than that might produce unreliable results, so try to move the process along relatively quickly depending on the number of clubs you want to test. A thorough process might necessitate two different sessions to select the best driver for you. On the other hand, if you already have your driver choice narrowed down, start your testing of clubs with a professional or representative of the manufacturing company immediately, focusing on clubhead loft, different shaft options and a specific setting for your driver.

The modern driver and ball are designed to launch high rather quickly, carry and stay in the air a long time and then fall to the turf without much *run-out* or roll. That is the reason most professionals use drivers with more loft than you would expect, usually 9.5 or 10.5 degrees of loft. If you prefer a more boring, lower flight shot (similar to an airplane take-off) that finishes with more roll, demo clubs with less loft such as 8.5 or 9.5 degrees. Shaft flex, torque, weight and length will also have a dramatic effect of a shot's trajectory, so work with one of the professionals or club representatives and try many different combinations to determine which combination of options produces the maximum results for you.

Ultimately, verifying the statistical information with the driver you select is an important thing to do, but it is equally important to have the correct settings of the driver fit for your particular stance and swing characteristics so that the club provides you with the best combination of launch, spin, distance, trajectory and accuracy. You can save time and money in the long run by consulting with a trusted professional during this process.

Fundamentals

Grip: Grip your driver with light pressure and a neutral grip— despite the length and overall size of this club, determining the proper grip is a delicate process because the main goal of the driver is to have a tight, controlled ball flight dispersion in order to eliminate missed fairways or worse. If you feel the club face is not rotating fast enough in the impact zone for a consistently square hit (for example, if the ball starts and stays or slices to the left of the target) then adjust both hands together in small increments to the left, or into a stronger grip position. Once you establish a grip that produces a *straight* ball flight with little or no side spin, take note of your hand position and try to replicate that grip throughout your practice session or round. Please note that this might be a unique grip position that you use exclusively for the driver, but it should remain your starting point for all driver swings.

When the shape of a hole requires or suggests that you move the ball from left to right or right to left, you should initially strengthen your grip for a left to right shot or draw, or weaken your grip for a right to left shot or fade. Changing your grip slightly will help you achieve the desired curvature of the ball. For some players the grip change alone is a sufficient adjustment to shape shots with your driver. Also, start with minor grip adjustments as a way to fix or correct consistently missed drives during a round on the course. In other words, if you hit a hooked drive that might be out of bounds, at least weaken your grip to the right a half inch to an inch before you play your provisional shot.

Some advanced players trust a specifically shaped shot for all relatively straight holes once they feel a high level of control with that shape. For most golfers, it is a right to left shot, or fade, where they aim the ball at a spot/target area on the right side of the fairway and put a small amount of right to left spin on the shot so the ball ends up in the middle of the fairway. This type of shot, a fade or small cut shot, is generally easier to control than a left to right spinning shot, a draw. Also, the ball usually lands softly with a fade and does not *run-out* or roll as much as it will with left to right spin once it hits the ground.

Alignment: The driver is one of the easiest clubs to get misaligned from your target. Remember, everything about the driver is big—it is the far end of the spectrum—so you have to be very careful when it comes to every fundamental and concept related to this club. Use the same alignment process for the driver that you use with every club—feet, knees, hips and shoulders lines are all square with each other and aimed at a spot parallel right of your ball target, except with this club, because the targets are so far away, you will need to establish your body lines target 10-12 yards to the right of your ball target. Find a feature of the hole in the landscape such as an edge of a bunker, a mound or a light or dark crisscross mower cut on the fairway, as your body aiming point.

Take your stance first setting your body lines square to that spot before you set the club in a playing position. Almost always you will need to make small adjustment steps closer to or further from the ball but be careful when you make these adjustment steps that you maintain lines of your feet, knees, hips and shoulders at the body's alignment aiming point, not the ball target. It is very common that during the adjustment steps that we realign ourselves incorrectly by shifting those body lines directly at the ball target. When your parallel body alignment lines lose their parallel right aspect and become convergent on the ball target, many issues arise related to the accuracy of the shot.

This alignment problem is the central cause for missing your target with driver swings. So, even though it is sometimes difficult to diagnose and correct problems/flaws on your own while playing, this is the place to start if you are missing your target consistently, hitting shots with undesired sidespin and not driving the ball in the fairway.

Stance/Set-up: In keeping with *all things being big* with the driver, your stance is the widest and most upright address position we use in any swing. Moreover, it requires you to be the most athletic in your swing and overall balance. Your feet should set-up slightly wider than your shoulders. Reduce your usual 60%-40% right-centered balance slightly back to a more evenly balanced ratio of 55%-45% or just enough on the lead leg and foot that you feel your weight centered on the right side but without any lean of your upper body to the right or left; a neutral posture will allow the coiling and uncoiling of the body to occur with proper sequencing and timing more often than not. Create a tall, upright posture with your forward spine tilt being shallower, or less than with any other club. Adopt a slight knee flex and bend forward from the hips into your spine tilt to insure proper stability in both parts of the swing.

Your back should be flat/straight without much arch, either negative or positive, in the lower back and without any *rounding* or *hunching* in the shoulder area and upper back. Also, keep the upper part of your spine in the neck area straight and tall; in other words, avoid tipping your head forward by maintaining about four inches between your chin and sternum.

Ball position for the driver is very important. Because the ball is on a tee an inch or so above the ground, the ball position must be very far forward of dead center—near the instep of your lead foot or the inside edge of your lead shoe. At address your lead arm is straight and in line with the club shaft without any forward press of the hands.

Driver ball position and wider stance

The upper arms and chest connection is minimal for the driver swing because the ball is so far away from you due to the length of the club, however it is still advised to maintain some connection in the arm pit area to maintain a sense of synchronicity and togetherness between the core muscles of the upper body and the small muscles of the arms and hands. The shoulders should be relatively level or neutral at address, not tilted with one shoulder lower or higher than the other. Your final hand position for the driver will be comfortably stretched-out away from your hips rather than hanging down from the shoulders. The club's overall length requires your hands to be in this relaxed, yet extended position approximately 12-14 inches from your belt buckle depending on your height and arm length.

Footwork: The lead foot should flare out slightly or open to the target by about 10-15 degrees in order to better accept your weight shift during the forward swing and follow through. The trail foot should be square to your ball target line. Your weight is evenly balanced under your shoe laces on the balls of your feet.

Also, in order to maintain maximum stability during the driver swing, try to spread your toes apart and press them down so they feel like they are *gripping* the turf. During the backswing, both heels should ideally stay on the ground and your weight should remain solidly under your shoe laces. If there is any movement in your footwork because of the length and force of the driver swing, it should only occur to the inside edges of your shoes and stay completely centered between your legs and shoulders; the same is true for your knees. Do not allow your trail leg knee to move to the outside edge of your trail shoe.

Some players like to feel their balance and center of gravity is in their mid-section or belt buckle area. Regardless, do not allow your weight shift to slide the trail knee outside of its original position or to the outside edge of the trail foot and shoe.

In the forward swing, have your legs and feet work as stabilizers for the hip and upper body rotation through the swing. Your connection with the ground is a key for maintaining balance, minimizing upper body movement either side to side (laterally) or up and down (vertically) and making solid contact with the ball. As your lead hip starts the forward swing after the point of transition by moving back and away from the ball, your trail foot will be activated by your overall weight to the lead side; simply allow the trail foot's heel to lift a little bit into and after the impact zone as you flow into your follow through position.

Backswing: The first move into the backswing with your driver should be a long, slow straight push back of the clubhead away from the ball initiated by the rotation of the chest.

This will be a *one-piece* movement if your upper arms are connected to the sides of your chest. Avoid the feeling that your hands are starting the club back; this can create a timing problem in the impact zone later in the swing. Your big or core muscles should control the major components of the swing as much as possible allowing your small muscles (arms and hands) to generate speed at the proper time in the swing. The connection between your upper arms and chest should create your natural swing plane. If you deliberately try to take the club back to the outside or inside it becomes easy to lose your arm/chest connection all together and allows your arms to take over the swinging of the club which usually ends up causing a sequencing error and timing problem at the critical point, impact.

The right arm stays straight in the backswing and your left arm will fold at the elbow. The left elbow should be no more than a few inches from your chest at the top of the backswing. Your hands should be as far away from your head as possible at the conclusion of the backswing, and ideally the shaft is close to parallel to the ground with a full wrist set. Your overall weight has remained balanced in a right-centered position.

Finish your backswing completely—make a full rotation of your chest and shoulders to the transition stopping point and *allow the entire club and rotational momentum to gather* before there is *any* movement by a part of your body into the forward swing. A major problem occurs is one part of your body is still moving in the direction of the backswing (usually the shoulders and arms) while another part of your body (usually the torso or upper body) starts to glide or slide in the opposite direction, thus beginning the forward swing. Obviously, this kind of disconnected movement between the two parts of the swing will be difficult to correct at impact. The synchronicity between all of the parts of the body first moving together in the backswing and then sequencing properly in the forward swing is the major swing key for the driver. You must coordinate the two movements as separate parts, each distinctly unified for proper timing and maximum energy transfer into the shot.

Forward Swing: Hopefully you are fully loaded or coiled at the transition point in a comfortable yet stretched position. Some people like to think of their muscles being pulled taut like an expanded rubber band and full of energy. The key in the forward swing is to release this tension in the correct sequence of movements so you maximize your clubhead speed at impact. The first move in the forward swing is the backward rotation of the lead hip away from the ball. Your head, shoulders and spine should retain a fairly constant position without shifting or sliding to the right. A sway to the right with the upper body will almost always produce an open club face into the impact zone resulting in a blocked shot to the left or a slicing ball flight because the club face is not square at impact. The opposite action will occur when you speed up your hand action in an attempt to have the club catch-up with your body which usually results in a smothered, hooking shot because the clubhead has over-rotated too quickly. Your chest should follow the right hip rotation in the downswing.

During this initial phase of the transition and the forward swing, hold your wrist angle and maintain your upper arm/chest connection. After your arms and hands reach waist height in the forward swing, your wrists and forearms will naturally activate accelerating the speed of the clubhead and squaring the face into the impact position.

As with all of your clubs, the six inches immediately following impact is the area of the swing where the club should be moving at its fastest speed. That part of the impact zone is when your hands are releasing the club and *cracking the whip,* so to speak. This represents the correct way to deliver the most energy into the shot while maintaining your overall balance and body coordination. Centrifugal force will cause your arms to be fully extended the first few feet following impact until your arm/chest connection naturally starts to fold your right, then left arm comfortably into your follow through position.

Follow Through: A full release of the hands and forearms and the rotation of the upper body and hips into the follow through position with the driver should be completed with your trail shoulder pointed at the target. If done properly, your chest rotation will actually go past your body alignment target by an additional 15-25 degrees.

Your hands will finish above your right shoulder and further to the right of it. After impact, your driver will be moving faster than any other club, however, if your upper and lower body flow together into the follow through, you should be able to complete the swing balanced on your lead foot and left toes with your upper body stable over the lead hip and leg. As always, you should be able to hold your final position with your belt buckle pointed at the target for a full three to five seconds.

Correct follow through position

Impact: Driver clubheads are big and forgiving. There is good energy transfer into the ball even when the ball is struck in the area near the sweet spot of the club face. However, maximum energy transfer occurs on shots hit directly in the center of the face. Hitting the ball consistently on this spot is complicated, because the ball is elevated on a tee and is so far forward near the lead foot in your stance; both elements that only happen with a driver. During a driver swing, the driver actually makes contact with the ball a few inches past the typical impact point for other clubs. Driver contact occurs *after* the bottom of the clubhead swing arc as the club is starting its upward and path to the right in the second or upward part of the arc near the end of the impact zone. This constitutes the beginning of the follow through. For impact to be consistently solid, the clubhead should be moving on a shallow or sweeping and slightly upward path rather than a descending or downward path.

To achieve this type of arc, stay neutrally centered during both parts of the swing and maintain an upright spine angle without dipping the lead shoulder or head toward the ball during your forward swing.

Always watch a very specific spot on the ball during your driver swing such as a dimple, letter or number. Create a routine position and focal point for the mark that you follow every time when you tee the ball. This is especially important when making a driver swing because the ball is so far away from your eyes and hands, is in a unique ball position in your stance, and is elevated off the turf. Try to focus your eyes on the spot throughout the swing and keep your eyes fixed on that mark until the ball disappears following impact.

How/What to Practice

Rhythm, timing, smooth tempo and solid contact are the big keys for the driver swing. All players have their own swing tempo related to the pace or speed of the swing. Regardless of your overall swing tempo, you should at least attempt to start the clubhead away from the ball slowly and keep your backswing unrushed and under control. Taking the driver back quickly or having a rapidly paced backswing has no relationship to your clubhead speed at impact. In fact for some golfers, a backswing with a fast tempo makes a controlled transition more difficult to achieve and can frustrate the goal of keeping your upper and lower body in concert during the forward swing.

The transition point in the driver swing is one of the important elements of the driver swing to spend time practicing on a regular basis. There should be no sense of urgency to change the direction of the club from backswing to forward swing. A small pause actually allows the momentum of the backswing and the clubs corresponding movement to gather together before the core muscles initiate the sequencing of the chain reaction of body parts of the forward swing.

Totally finish your backswing before any part of your body moves to the right beginning the forward swing. The *hold 2 drill* is a great practice routine to use with your driver—complete the backswing and stop; hold that position for a *full two seconds* before rotating the lead hip backwards away from the ball to start the forward swing. This initial move after the transition point should be done in an unhurried manner. Once the hips start to rotate, your mid-section, chest and shoulders will follow naturally in succession—your arms, wrists, hands and the club will be the final elements to uncoil. If you maintain your wrist set in the beginning half of the forward swing, you will create abundant energy and speed with the club as it moves into and through the impact zone. Then the final goal is to hit the ball in the center of the club face in order to achieve *your* ultimate energy transfer and ball speed.

During your practice sessions and while playing holes on the golf course, always pick a ball target for your shot and a body alignment spot that is parallel right of that ball target. Find a reliable grip and stance that promotes a consistently tight ball dispersion within 10-12 yards of either right or left of your ball target with your driver swing. A tight dispersion is 20-25 yards wide with the ball target being located in the center of that area. Once you feel comfortable with your driver swing performance, practice shaping slight right to left fades or small left to right draws into that same 25 yard space.

Start this process with a minor grip change either weakening or strengthening your grip and verify the effect on your ability to curve the ball by imparting subtle amounts of spin. The second technique you might implement to shape shots is to change your stance. You can open your stance by dropping your lead foot back a few inches or close your stance by moving it in front of your trail foot by two to three inches. When you change your stance, also change your other alignment lines—knees, hips and shoulders to match the line of your toes. Make these changes in small increments while you experiment with techniques that help you shape shots with your driver. Control and accuracy are the concepts you are adding to distance and power.

Once you are able to blend all four of these driver characteristics together on a consistent basis, you will have mastered the driver swing. Your game will elevate to a new level, and you will enjoy playing competitive rounds because the shot hit with the driver *sets the stage* for the rest of the hole.

Drills for the Driver

Swoosh drill: Turn your driver upside down and grip it on the shaft near the clubhead with your usual grip. The grip is down, near the turf. Make slow backswings and in the forward swing gradually increase the speed of the grip end near the typical impact zone of the swing. You will hear a *swooshing* sound at the bottom of the swing arc. Finish these practice swings on balance and repeat the drill at least ten times.

Then take a right handed stance and perform the *swoosh drill* right-handed ten times. This promotes muscle balance and coordination on both sides of your body.

Clip the tee drill: Take your driver stance focusing on all of your driver swing fundamentals. Place a tee in the ground in the proper ball position spot for a driver, but do not place a ball on the tee. Take a swing focusing on a smooth rhythm and transition and try to hit or clip the top part of the tee with your driver. Usually the tee will lift and spin out of the ground if you hit just the top part of the tee. Your eyes should focus on the round, top portion of the tee during the drill. Check your driver face occasionally. You should see an impression or mark left by the tee. It should only be on the bottom 1/2 inch of the driver face where you could image the ball above it on the sweet spot. Also, check this tee mark on your driver's club face while you are playing rounds or practicing on the course; it provides you with good feedback and suggests possible adjustments in your ball position, stance or simply the height you tee the ball above the turf. Repeat the drill five times.

Finish and Hold Drill: Hit practice drives making fundamentally sound swings and concentrating on all of the concepts you are trying to master in your driver swing. Hold your final follow through position or pose for a full three seconds or until the ball lands. This is one of the key drills you can actually use on the course while playing a round of golf if you are experiencing difficulties with your driver. Take practice swings while you are waiting to hit your tee shots—make smooth practice swings and hold your finish position to rehearse the proper fundamentals just before it is your turn to play.

Repeat five to ten times.

50% Swing Drill: Hit five practice drives with your driver swinging the club at only 50%-60% of your maximum swing speed. Grip the club lightly and watch the ball closely to emphasize solid ball striking. Repeat the drill hitting five shots at 75% of your maximum swing speed again concentrating on your balance and hitting the ball in the center of the club face. Too often we swing our clubs with the same effort level; usually close to our maximum speed. Practicing and hitting shots at lower clubhead speeds can teach us how to control the club with more proficiency and to hit the ball more closely to the center of the club face. Hitting shots with less speed reduces the spin you impart on the ball which is a very important skill to possess when playing in windy conditions or when playing shots at yardages that are less than your maximum distances with a particular club.

Play Holes Drill: At the end of your practice sessions, pretend to play the first six holes of your home course or the course you are playing that day if it is a warm-up session. Hit the first full swing shot and an approximated approach shot for each hole. Hopefully, you will hit a driver and then an iron; next a driver and a different iron; next a driver and a hybrid or fairway metal; and so on—the point of this drill in to alternate clubs of different types and lengths one after another so you are forced to make the changes to your stance, ball position and swing fundamentals as you are required to do while playing holes on the course during a round.

Checklist/Video: Have a friend or family member take photos or film a short video of your swing from directly behind you, or down the target line. In the pre-swing phase, check your parallel right body alignment; remember with the driver your feet, knees, hips and shoulders should be square to each other and aimed at a spot 10-12 yards parallel right of you ball target. Review the video and look for the following elements to be in place:

- tall posture—upright stance with a slight knee flex;
- a straight back and neck (entire spine not curved) with a neutral spine;
- chin elevated three or four inches from your chest; and
- hand position further away from your hips than with other clubs—approximately 10-12 inches from your belt buckle but arms not stretched too far away from your body.

Ask the person taking the video to also take pictures or record a few videos from the side facing directly at you. Check for the following pre-swing positions from the face-on angle:

- weight balanced on the lead side slightly (a feeling of 55%-45% but probably less);
- lead foot toes flared open toward the target about 10-15 degrees;
- right arm straight and in line with the shaft of the club with little or no forward press of the hands;
- ball position just inside the instep or arch of the lead shoe; and
- the ball teed up approximately 1 and 1/4 inches off the turf—experiment with different heights to determine the best position for your swing attack angle.

Verify the effects that different teeing heights have on your driver's ball flight, trajectory and roll-out and select one that favors your desired results. During the driver swing review the photos or video from this angle for the following positions:

- the club starts back away from the ball *low and slow* and initiated by the rotation of the chest;
- the toe of the driver pointed up at the sky when your hands reach waist height;
- the wrist set occurs somewhat early during the backswing and the wrists are fully set (90 degrees) at the top of the backswing;
- shaft is approximately parallel to the ground and pointed down the target line at the transition point;
- spine tilt is maintained in the starting stance position during the backswing;
- the arm/chest connection is maintained during the backswing;
- right arm is straight and rigid and left elbow is bent and only a few inches from your chest at the top of the backswing;
- the forward swing begins with a backward rotation of the lead hip with only a small hip slide to the right before the hips start to rotate and clear;
- check your balance has remained stationary in a right-centered position and your feet are flat on the ground without your weight rolling to the edges of your shoes;
- retain your wrist set as long as possible in the forward swing;
- verify that the transition was smooth, unhurried and initiated by the rotation of the core muscles of the upper body not the arms and hands (especially the dominant trail arm and hand pulling the club down and attempting to *hit* the ball with extra force);
- at the impact position the entire body—weight, core, arms—and club are synchronized at a straight lead side with the arms fully extended and the trail foot heel lifting slightly off the ground;
- finish the rotation of your hips and chest past the ball target line so your left shoulder is pointing at the target and the right shoulder is behind your face; and
- hold your follow through, on balance with your belt buckle and face squarely at the target.

Fitness/Exercise *Always consult with your doctor before starting any exercise program. The fitness/exercise suggestions in this book should be used only by golfers in good health. Use common sense, adapt the suggestions to fit your current health concerns, or skip these sections if appropriate. Stop immediately if you experience any pain or discomfort and check with your physician.*

Basic Yoga Stretches and Poses: Research yoga routines online or in a bookstore. Look for basic standing and dynamic yoga exercise routines. Perform the poses very slowly—1/3 of the time moving into the pose or stretch, 1/3 of the time holding the pose or stretch and 1/3 of the time releasing out of the stretch and returning to your initial position. This type of movement should take approximately 30 seconds total. Focus on exercises that combine core strength building, flexibility and balance. At first these routines may seem easy. You will probably be surprised at how much they activate your muscles and force you to exert yourself. Do yoga exercises as often as possible, hopefully every day. A great time to do this part of your fitness routine is while watching television.

Leg Swings: (variation 1) Stand a few feet from a wall or counter, straighten and swing one leg from the hip joint back and forth (to the left and then to the right) in front and past your body in a sideways manner. Your toes face the wall or counter and you can touch the surface with your hands for balance as you swing the leg a few feet past the center position in both directions. Do ten leg swings then switch legs and repeat the exercise. During these leg swings try to maintain the same height with your body and head by flexing the knee of your stable leg; in other words, try not to rise up or drop down as your leg is swinging.

(variation 2) Stand sideways or parallel to the same wall or counter and swing one leg forward and backward—your legs will swing a little further in this variation than in the sideways variation. Again, try to maintain a steady height during these swings; perform ten swings with each leg.

Two Arm Swings: Take your driver stance with your weight right-centered at a ratio of 60%-40% and let your arms hang down naturally and relaxed and under your shoulders. Rotate your upper body and arms to about the halfway position of your backswing with your arms separated by about 12 inches. Feel the left hip turn straight back a few inches. Now rotate your body and arms to the right side or your body about halfway into your forward swing by pulling the right hip back and away from your toes. Repeat the exercise ten times. Try to focus on the feeling of the correct movement of the hips as they are coordinated with the upper body rotation of the golf swing. Your upper arms should stay connected with your chest and you should feel the speed created in arms and hands by centrifugal force as you rotate into the forward swing portion of the exercise.

Weight Training: With a weighted ball or your pair of dumbbells, perform a clean and jerk; the weighted object slightly off the ground below your knees as you squat with a straight back; your feet are about 12-15 inches apart and your arms are extended hanging straight down from your shoulders. In one smooth, but explosive movement, rise out of the squat by pushing down with your toes and balls of the feet to a standing position. At the same time, lift the weight by raising your arms so the weights finish in front of your chest and shoulder area. Repeat ten times—this exercise activates your entire posterior chain of muscles and is a great way to train for strength and flexibility or to do as a warm-up activity. As always, start with a light amount of weight that you can handle easily and over time gradually increase the weight. To avoid injuries, use reasonable, lighter weights and a total number of repetitions that does strain your muscles or joints and does not overtax your body in general. Weight training is very important part of an exercise and fitness program needed to build the strength and stability you must possess for a successful golf swing.

Chapter 5 The Putter

The single most important scoring club in your bag, bar none, is your putter. Yet most of us don't practice our putting nearly as much as we practice with our other clubs. Frankly, this is because we don't get the same level of satisfaction of hitting a great putt as we do when we hit a good shot with virtually any other club. We can hit a drive 250 and miss our target by 25 yards and accept it as a successful shot because it is still on the fairway. Our approach shot to a green might be 20 feet from our target but because we hit the green in regulation we consider our approach a successful shot. However, when a 12 foot birdie putt misses the hole we inevitably deem the shot unsuccessful.

There are several reasons why we regard putting in such a harsh light. First of all, putting is much harder than it looks. This lowers our expectations because we are rarely successful on our attempts from beyond three or four feet. Second, the fact that any stroke with a putter, even if it is a tap-in putt from one inch from the hole, counts equally with any other full swing shot just seems unfair and obviously, produces an unpleasant feeling. And nothing in golf stings more or is as demoralizing as a 3-putt green. So what can we do about it?

We can start by embracing putting as golf's ultimate challenge of our intelligence, fine motor skills and ability to control our emotions and nerves. Confidence plays a big part of playing golf well, as does self-discipline, logical thinking, self-control and execution. In putting, there is little margin for error—our alignment, ball speed, read of the green and the combination of these elements executed in the proper stoke must be nearly flawless. Most of us underestimate how precise our attention to detail must be when we make a putter swing. Oftentimes, we impatiently adopt a *hit and hope* mentality and accordingly, miss most of our putts. Over time it is easy to develop a defeatist attitude toward this part of the game, because we are so rarely successful in it by our own standards.

Almost half of the strokes we play during a round of golf are with our putter. Common sense tells us that putting demands a greater priority than most of the other swings in golf. If we can develop the proper attitude of respect and embrace the opportunity that putting affords us, we can turn what is arguably the most dreaded part of the game into one of our strengths.

Let's face it, we are all equal regardless of age, strength, size, gender or experience when it comes to holding and using a putter, which is not the case with so many other clubs in our bag. The fact that a one inch putt counts the same as a 275 yard drive is one of the ironic symmetries of golf and a reason why putting has been labeled as *the great equalizer* in the sport.

Key Points for Putting: Q & A

What do I need to know about the different types and styles of putters when I select the best putter for me?

We all have a natural putting stroke. If your arms are connected to your chest, your stroke will go inside in the backswing, return to square in the impact zone and will go inside again in the forward swing and follow through. This type of stroke is commonly referred to as a *swinging gate or arced* stroke. On the other hand, if you take the putter straight back and straight through on your ball target line, you have a *square to square* putting stroke. Manufacturers make specific models of putters that match each of these two strokes. If you have a *swinging gate or arced* stroke, your putter should have the shaft entering the head somewhere near the heel of the putter.

Conversely, if you have a square to square putting stroke, your putter should be face-balanced. These putters are usually designed with the shaft connected near the center of the putter head. You should first determine which type of putting stroke is natural for you, and then match your putter to your stroke. There is a simple test you can perform on any putter to establish which of the two styles (toe-hang design or face-balanced design) the putter is and whether it is appropriate for your stroke. Ask a PGA Professional for assistance, or research the test on-line, so that you can both verify your type of stroke and find a putter that will complement your putting rather that work in an opposite direction.

There are so many variables to consider when selecting a putter; which ones are the most important?

There are many variables so the following items are some of the most important elements that you should consider:

Forgiveness—Almost all of the putters made in the past 20 years have been designed with *extra heel and toe weighting* and an *open cavity* behind the sweet spot of the putter face. This design is more forgiving in that it makes the sweet spot of the putter bigger than the sweet spot on an older, solid blade style putter. The larger sweet spot area improves the energy transfer of the club into the ball on slightly miss-hit putts. This design feature comes in many shapes and sizes, so you should be able to find a putter head that appeals to your eye and allows you to take advantage of this type of forgiveness.

Inserts: The purpose of all inserts is to make the contact between the club and the ball feel *soft* to you in varying degrees. The only other way to control the contact-feel of a putt is to use a golf ball with a soft cover. Spend some time finding the ball that feels best with *your* putter but also performs the way you want it to from tee to green.

Feel is a very important variable in putting because it helps you gauge the speed of the green and control the distance of your putts. Inserts also have an effect on the *sound* made when impact occurs. Pay careful attention to both variables when experimenting with putters and try to find the combination that feels and sounds best to you. Most professionals considering equipment changes find it much easier to change clubs than to change from one ball to another, whereas most amateurs fail to consider the impact playing with different balls can have on their putting results.

Lengths: Your natural putting stance, your physical characteristics regarding height and arm length and your desired arm hang or position during your putter swing will determine the proper length of your putter. Most players fit into a 34" or a 35" putter, but it is a good idea to work with a golf professional you trust to verify your correct putter length through a proper fitting.

Grips: (variable 1) The shape, material and size of the actual grip on your putter makes a difference in how your hands control and square the putter. The smaller the grip the more your wrists and hands will be activated during the stroke. Conversely, oversized and "jumbo" putter grips are designed to minimize your wrist and hand action in the stroke. Generally speaking, players with swinging gate strokes should use conventional or midsize grips while players with square to square putting strokes can use conventional, midsize or larger grips, depending on their preference of feel.

(variable 2) The grip with which your hands hold the club can have many variations. *Conventional, right hand low and the claw* are just a few common options. Either of the first two grips is preferable because you will probably swing the putter more consistently the same way when your hands are together and can work as a single unit rather than separated as in the claw grip. The one thing almost all putter grips have in common is that they attempt to minimize wrist and hand influence in the stroke. Swinging the putter with the rocking of the shoulders is the best way to repeat an effective putter stroke.

Head Style—Blade or Mallet: It stands to reason that a *mallet headed putter*, because of its larger size and shape, is easier to control and keep stabilized during a stroke than is a *blade style putter* which usually has a thin design. Try both types and test for a difference in performance results as well as assessing the difference in feel and design appeal. You might simply view a mallet style as clumsy or strange looking and if the results don't merit that selection, select your putter using another hierarchy of criteria that makes sense to you. Like most equipment options, there is no one right or wrong choice of a putter. You should filter your selection through a myriad of options (some of which we just covered) and set your own priorities related to looks, feel, sound and performance.

Ultimately, the putter that produces the best results is the one you should select because your goal with this club is to use it as little as possible. Factoring in all of the different variables is the recommended way to select the putter that inspires your confidence and provides the control you need to start the ball on the line you select and at the speed you are attempting to produce.

Weight: A putter head with a heavier swing-weight or feel is easier to control than a putter head with a lighter swing-weight. However, feel, speed and distance control, especially on short putts is more difficult with a heavier putter simply because the extra weight transfers more energy into the ball. Putters designed with extra weight in the heel and toe of the putter head have a slightly larger sweet spot and maintain a more stable face during the stroke and through impact with the ball. Heel-toe weighting almost always coincides with an open cavity behind the sweet spot of the ball. You can find examples heel-toe weighting in both mallet and blade style putters and some of these putters will open and close during the putter swing while other putters might be face balanced and remain square during your putter swing. Experimentation is necessary to determine a specific putter's effectiveness for you.

Fundamentals

Grip: Feel and touch are very important elements in any precise activity, whether painting, typing, cooking or putting. You should grip the putter a similar hand position that you use in gripping all of your other clubs; that is with your hands connected to one another and with the left hand low. Overall, this provides you with the best feel for controlling putts of varying distances and promotes a consistent stance/set-up position and an athletic movement throughout your round.

Standard reverse-overlap putting grip

Grip pressure should always be very light and relaxed in your putter swing. The reverse overlap grip is the most widely used grip to connect the hands. Both palms should be in neutral positions, facing each other and both thumbs should rest on the center or top of the grip in line with each other. It is important to achieve passive hand neutrality so your dominant hand doesn't rotate the club face too quickly or slowly or become too active and *hits* at the ball.

However, some players find a disruption of the customary grip useful when experiencing putting woes. If you feel a change is necessary because of a putting slump, practice putting using the *right hand low* grip or the *claw* grip. It will confuse your muscles and quiet your wrists and hands while creating a positive pendulum stroke that originates with your shoulders. Unfortunately, the improvement this grip makes in the actual putter swing is typically offset by a lack of feel and loss of distance control, at least initially.

Alignment: The alignment of your feet, knees, hips and shoulders in putting should be parallel right but with these shortest of golf shots, at the smallest amount, approximately six to twelve inches to the right of your ball target line. Your body alignment should be very square on your body alignment line at a specific spot or target on the putting surface. If any of the four body alignment lines are not square to one another, the chances of making the putt greatly diminish. The smallest of margins, three degrees, two degrees, or even one degree of misalignment results in the ball rolling inches off the target line.

Not aiming the putter correctly or not squaring the club face at impact are the most common reasons we miss putts, but the misalignment of one or more of our body lines can predetermine a missed putt, regardless of the quality of the stoke. Misalignment of a body lines usually happens when we set our feet line directly at the hole rather than at a spot parallel right of the ball target or when we open our shoulders to the right of the target as we look up at the hole in final preparation of making the stroke.

Pick your body alignment target or spot, square all four of your body lines to that target and maintain that pre-swing address position and posture until you start the putter in motion. After your stance is set, then aim the putter face directly at your intended ball target or on the line you need to get the ball rolling on based on your read of the green variables of a specific putt. If you need to make adjustments to your stance in that part of the pre-swing process of the putt, make sure to square *all* of your body alignment lines to that adjusted spot, not just your feet lines.

Stance/Set-up: In putting, you should resume the 60%-40% right-centered balance ratio with more of your static weight on the lead leg and foot. This set-up will stabilize your body from swaying left to right or right to left during the putter swing. Your weight should be balanced in the center of your feet under your shoe laces; not too far forward on your toes and not too far back on your heels and not on the outside or inside edges of your shoes. You should have a slight knee flex, again to help maintain your stability, and your back and neck (full spine) should be straight and neutral without being tense. Your chin should be up, three to four inches from your chest, and generally, your stance should feel somewhat tall and upright. Your arms will hang directly under your shoulders in a relaxed position that leaves your hands in a final position that is closer to your belt buckle than with any other club—only a few inches from your belt. The upper halves of your arms down to the elbows should lightly touch or connect to the sides of your rib cage. The ideal ball position is slightly forward of center, about an inch or two inside your lead heel and the heel of your putter should be directly under your eyes and only a few inches in front of your toes.

Footwork: During a putter swing your feet will stay flat on the ground, your weight is centered under the shoe laces (on the balls of your feet) and your weight distribution is at 60% on your lead leg and foot. Find a comfortable width for your feet, probably closer together than the feet positions for your other swings unless you have a very long putt that demands a long swing of the putter. Obviously, there should be very little movement below the waist in a putter swing and virtually none of the footwork concerns of the other full swings. While putting, your feet must be aligned squarely and correctly parallel to a spot right of your ball target line and the hole. Your feet provide a sturdy connection to the turf that allows your upper body to swing the putter back and through without much if any lateral, upward or downward movement.

Backswing: Assuming your pre-swing fundamentals are in order, the backswing starts the substantive part of successful putting. You must develop a trigger that starts the putter in motion in a smooth and consistent fashion. Whenever you are performing any detail work in life that requires precision and touch, such as throwing a dart, threading a needle or painting, you would naturally use your dominant hand. Some players feel confident pulling the putter in motion with the dominant hand or initiating the shoulder pendulum rock of the shoulders.

Other players prefer a sensation of *pushing back* the putter with the lead hand or starting the shoulder action with the feeling that lead upper arm and shoulder start the movement. In either case, the *trigger* will be the big muscles of the shoulders or your small muscles of your hands. Experiment trying both triggers—try the big muscles of your shoulders with the feeling of either the lead or trail shoulder starting the movement with your hands passive and only serving as the connectors to the putter. In this stroke, the arms and putter form a one piece unit that is swung by the rocking of the shoulders. The second technique involves using your small muscles to initiate the backswing by either pulling the putter back with your dominant hand or pushing the putter back with your lead hand.

My preference is using the small muscles because it favors the sensitivity, touch and feel that is needed for detail work. Test both systems thoroughly and determine which performs best for you, and then make a conscious effort to use that trigger to start the putter in motion on every putt. Some players use a small forward press of the hands to start the putter in motion. Experiment with this technique as well as a consistent way to begin the stroke.

If you look at putters closely, you will notice that the height or depth of the putter face is rather small; in fact, almost all putter faces are shorter than the ball. So, our first priority is to hit the ball in the sweet spot of the putter face. In order to accomplish this goal, you must do one or a combination of two things—first, you can make contact with the ball past the bottom of the putter swing arc or on the initial part of the follow through; this is likely to happen if you have the ball positioned far enough forward of center. The second option is to *lift or hold* the putter head a small amount (1/4 -1/2 of an inch) above the ground before starting the backswing. Technically, the second option would be the initial move in the backswing and should be performed with the dominant hand.

Path is the second key element of the backswing portion of the putter swing. You should try to make a stroke with the putter moving straight back and through impact on the ball target line. If you chose the dominant hand trigger, the feeling in your hand should be to *pull* the putter away from the ball for your backswing and then to *push* it into the forward swing through impact and into the follow through. Try not to pay attention to how the putter face is moving during the stroke. A swinging gate putter is designed for the toe to open in the backswing, return to square at impact and close during the forward swing, whereas a face balanced putter should remain square to the ball target line throughout the stroke. Keep your eyes focused on the back of the ball where the club will make contact with the ball rather than watching the putter head, even with your peripheral vision.

One of the most common mistakes players make is not taking the putter back far enough in the backswing and then trying to make-up for the lack of energy by *hitting* the putt with their dominant hand. Try to think of the putter swing as a *putting stroke*, not a *putting hit*.

Forward Swing: The transition between the backswing and the forward swing is perhaps the most important transition point in any of the five swings. Because the stroke is so short, there is little time or space to make a correction if a putter transition gets the putter moving on a wrong path or at an uneven pace going into the impact zone. Try to feel the putter swing to a stopping point on the backswing—this is sometimes described as a gathering of momentum. Then feel gravity and the opposite (or reverse) momentum start to *smoothly swing* the putter back to the ball on the forward swing.

Your dominant hand *pulls* the putter back and then starts the putter forward with gravity and a gentle *push*. Just like every other club, the putter should gradually gather speed on the forward swing into impact, although it is obviously far less than in other full swings; but the same principles apply. The putter actually stops moving in one direction and then transitions into movement in the other direction.

It is a small swinging of the club, yet it is still a golf *swing*. Throughout the putter swing, keep the top or butt end of the putter grip pointed at the center of your mid-section, almost as if you were using a long putter anchored into your stomach. Both ends of the putter must be free to move but there are advantages to limiting the overall movement of the grip end of the club. This will activate your wrists to move to some extent during the swing, especially on longer putts. Simply allow the dominant hand and wrist to control the stroke and swinging the putter. Also, be aware that the putter head will swing past your hands in both directions—behind them in the backswing and in front of them in the forward swing. Limit the movement of your head, spine and core muscles in putting. Your head should not move laterally in the swing, and keep your feet flat on the ground during your putting stroke. Maintain a 60%-40% right-centered balance as the key for eliminating movement of any kind in the swing.

Follow Through: Always extend your putter head down the ball target line toward the hole or aiming spot; that constitutes the proper follow through position in putting. As with a metronome or pendulum, the putter head should ideally swing an equal distance past the point of impact with the ball as it swung behind the ball in the backswing. In other words, if a 15 foot putt requires a ten inch backswing to propel the ball the proper distance to the target, then you should also swing it ten inches past impact in the forward swing for a total of 20 inches for the full stroke. Also, point your putter head at the hole or target as your final follow through position, the way you point your belt buckle at your target at the end of a full swing with any other club.

Impact: One of the most undervalued concepts in putting is making perfect contact or impact with the ball. The sweet spot on a putter is small, but the stroke is so short that it should be a conscious priority for you to hit every putt *solidly on the center of the club face*. The transfer of energy from the putter is maximized into the ball when you hit the ball with the sweet spot. The ball will hold the intended line better, roll end over end with less side spin and travel closer to the intended distance when the energy transfer is at its best. Some players look at a dimple on the top of the ball or focus on the spot of impact on the back of the ball while making a putting stroke. Just make sure your putter's sweet spot is directly behind that impact point before your start the putter in motion, and try to swing the putter back to the ball striking it with the center of the clubhead; the center or sweet spot is usually marked on the top edge of the putter with a dot or a sight line.

The best struck putts will *roll* smoothly and directly at the hole in much the same way that a perfectly struck full swing shot will fly in a tight trajectory directly at the target or flagstick. Think of your stroke as an attempt to *roll* the ball on the putting surface, not just *striking* the ball. The loft on the putter is designed to get the ball *rolling* as quickly as possible without bouncing or hopping along the ground. Putts that bounce quickly off the putter usually finish short of the hole, because of energy loss, whereas putts that get started *rolling* at the target have better energy transfer and will finish closer to the target or hole.

How/What to Practice

Accuracy and distance are the two key variables you must master to become an excellent putter.

Accuracy: The first test of accuracy is to be able to start the ball rolling on the ball target line. All of your putter swing fundamentals must be in order to give yourself the best chance for success, and your aim with the putter must be absolutely correct. Some players pick a spot six to ten inches in front of the ball such as a mark on the green or a patch of grass that is a different color and try to roll the ball over that spot. Mark a straight chalk (plumb) line on the practice green about three or four feet into the center of a hole. Place a ball six inches from the end of the line so you can follow the chalk line in the backswing and forward swing. The goal is to keep the ball rolling on the chalk line all the way into the hole.

This is an important practice drill so you know you can aim the putter correctly to a specific spot in the center of the hole and then make a stroke that starts the ball rolling on that line with proper over spin.

Another way to practice your accuracy with the putter is to pick a spot on the apex of a sloping line that is the point where you think gravity and the slope of the surface will start to move the ball either left to right or right to left; sometimes this is called the high point or apex of the putt. Roll a putt directly at that spot on the green. This is a good way to practice your putting accuracy and a good way to verify and hone your green-reading skills. In other words, if you think a ten foot putt will break three inches to the left on its path to the hole, pick a target or apex point three inches to the left of the hole that you think is the spot that the ball will start to turn toward the hole because of the slope and gravity. That spot or apex point is now your ball target and the path to that spot is the correct path or putting line for the putt. This is called spot putting.

Spend time working on this technique as a calculation for hitting putts correctly that include break and demand proper speed to go in the hole.

Distance Control/Speed: Go to a practice green with three or four balls of the type you regularly use. Start by rolling putts from a relatively long distance across the green from approximately thirty feet trying to get the ball to stop at the correct distance, even with the hole. As you practice, gradually reduce the distance from 25 to 20 to 15 feet and occasionally return to a set of putts from 30 feet, so that you train your eye-hand coordination to match effectively with your muscles to swing your putter with the proper force to roll the ball to different distances. From thirty feet or more, your goal should be to stop the ball within a three foot circle around the hole. From 20-25 feet your goal should tighten to stopping the ball within a two foot circle. From 15 feet or less, your goal should be to make the putt or to have the ball finish no more than one foot from the hole.

On putts from four feet or more, always aim for an imaginary hole 6-12 inches beyond the actual hole and on the same target line; the putt should simply roll directly over, and hopefully into, the actual hole on its way to your imagined hole because both holes are part of the same ball line. Shorter putts, say within four feet, should be aimed at a specific spot on the back edge of the hole, or just beyond the hole if the putt is sloped uphill. On an uphill putt, pick a target spot a few inches past the hole on the same line as the hole. Stick a tee in the ground three to six inches beyond or past the hole and use it as your aiming point while practicing, again allowing the actual hole to be on the ball's path to the tee. You will probably be surprised how many times the ball barely gets to the hole. Sometimes you might have misjudged the speed of the putt, but more often, a putt that stops short of your intended target is the result of a loss of energy that occurs because of an off-center strike on the putter face.

Practice uphill, downhill, and side hill putts of left to right and right to left slopes and of varying lengths to develop a feel for both speed and distance control. The first business in approaching any putt is to align your body lines at a spot parallel right of the intended line of the putt and then aim your putter directly and carefully at the ball target. This pre-swing task is one of the most important aspects in making putts. Once your lines and final address position have been established, shift your focus on the aiming spot for the putt and then on the overall speed and distance of the putt. The concept of accuracy through proper alignment of your body and the aim of your putter is your first concern, and distance control and the speed of the putt is your second concern.

Drills for Putting

Snow Sticks: Place two snow sticks or two golf clubs on the putting surface parallel to each other and about five or six inches apart so they form a *channel* for you to roll putts through. Place a ball in the middle, between the sticks so that you practice keeping the putter moving between them on both the backswing and the forward swing. Make the putter swings from about five or six feet from a hole and place a tee a few inches beyond the hole as your ball aiming spot. Finish each stroke with the putter head pointed directly at the tee.

Repeat 20 times from different angles at the hole.

Snow sticks putting drill

Left Hand Only: Practice putts from three to six feet holding the club with only your dominant hand. You will develop added feel for controlling the clubhead (that is 30 inches from your hand) for both accuracy and distance. Your hand should be in the same location on the grip as it would be if you were using two hands. A more challenging variation to this drill is to place two tees in the ground just wide enough for your putter to stroke through similar to a tight gate. Place the ball in the center of the space between the tees and swing the putter between the tees hitting only the ball; this forces you to control the clubhead of the putter on a straight path of as you swing it back and forth between the tees.

Once in a while, move to a place 15-20 feet from a hole and hit a few putts with the dominant hand only grip. On the shorter putts focus specifically on accuracy and on the longer putts focus on speed and distance control. This drill trains the dominant hand to control the putter in order to master both concepts of putting—accuracy and distance control. Repeat the drill from different distances for 20 total putts.

Lift, Pull, Push Drill: Practice six to eight foot putts with your focus on the three actions of the dominant hand—first lifting the putter head slightly off the ground; second pulling the putter into the motion of the backswing; and third pushing the putter head into its swinging motion of the forward swing. Allow the putter head to swing past your hands on both sides of the ball while pointing the end of the putter grip constantly at your mid-section as if it were anchored in your stomach. Try to develop feel of the putter head's weight and natural momentum during its swinging action. Repeat 20 times.

Small Hole Drill: Practice putting to a round object smaller than a hole such as another ball, a quarter, a divot repair tool or a tee stuck in the ground. Use this drill to refine your accuracy on short putts to its sharpest point of precision. This drill is perfect for one to four foot putts, and you can do the drill anywhere on the practice green regardless of the where the holes are cut. Your focus is to select the proper line for the target and to start the ball rolling on that line for the three or four feet. Practice this drill every day for 25-50 putts even if indoors on a carpet. You will build the skill and unwavering confidence you need on the golf course to make putts near the hole and your scores are guaranteed to improve. While playing competitive rounds, select a specific spot on an edge of the hole (usually a point on the back edge of the hole), imagine your practice object (tee or divot repair tool) and replicate the honed eye-hand coordination and muscle memory that you have ingrained through hundreds of practice repetitions.

Circle Drill: Space six balls around a hole in a circle, in the clock face positions of 12 o'clock, 2 o'clock, 4 o'clock, 6 o'clock, 8 o'clock and 10 o'clock and all at a specific distance, say three feet. Stroke all six putts and when you successfully make all six consecutively, repeat the drill from four feet around the hole. Once you make all six balls in succession from this distance repeat the drill again at five feet and then six feet. Try to find a hole that is cut in the practice green with various types of slope around it, so you can practice uphill, downhill, and side hill putts that combine the need for accuracy and speed control. Complete the drill one time from all four distances.

Line Drill: On the practice green place six balls in a straight line. Space the balls in 12 inch increments at progressive distances away from the hole. The first ball is three feet away, the second four feet away, and so on up to the last ball at eight feet away. After you make all six putts in succession, repeat the drill from a different angle at the hole and from a different set of distances, this time starting with the closest ball at five feet away and the final ball at ten feet from the hole. Once you make all six putts in a row, repeat the drill one more time, again from a different angle and this time with the closest ball starting at eight feet from the hole. In this sequence, try to make as many putts as possible from eight to thirteen feet.

25 Foot Putt Drill: Stroke six long putts from approximately 25 feet from a practice hole. The goal is to have all six balls finish no more than 18-24 inches from the hole. Once you achieve this goal, repeat the drill to a different hole location stroking all six balls and this time with the goal of having the balls finish within 12-18 inches from the hole.

Statistical Drill: Develop a putting chart where you record the number of putts you make from five different distances— three feet, four feet, six feet, ten feet and 15 feet. Once a week, hit five putts from each of the five distances and record how many putts you make from each location. Do this drill throughout your primary golf season or for at least three months. It is one of the best ways to track your progress and improvement and to determine if your putting practice is translating into lower scores in your competitive rounds.

Checklist/Video: Ask a friend or family member to take several photos or videos of you putting, both from behind (down the line) and face-on. Review the images for the following fundamentals:

- check for parallel right alignment, 6-12 inches from the hole on short putts and a little farther to the right on longer putts;
- check that your body lines—feet, knees, hips and shoulders—are all square to your alignment target;
- check your static weight balance is distributed at 60% on your lead side and remains stable during your putter swings;
- check your stance for an upright posture with a straight back and neck, chin up from your chest and your knees slightly flexed;
- check your hand position, which should be close to your belt buckle with your arms hanging comfortably straight down from your shoulders;
- check your ball position to verify from behind that the ball is in line directly under your eyes and from face on that the ball is positioned slightly forward of the center of your stance;
- the putter moves straight back away from the ball on the backswing and no part of your body moves to the laterally until the putter completely stops at the transition point;
- the putter's transition starts with the gravitational pull of the clubhead and a gentle push of the dominant hand so the putter swings smoothly toward the ball picking-up incremental speed through impact relative to the distance of the putt;

- check the end of the putter grip to see if it stays pointed at your midsection throughout the swing and that the putter head swings past your hands on both the backswing and forward swing;
- check that your shoulders and head do not move laterally or up and down; and
- check the follow through to see if the putter traveled an equal distance or number of inches on both sides of the ball and that the putter is pointed at the ball target and the end of the stroke.

Fitness/Exercises *Always consult with your doctor before starting any exercise program. The fitness/exercise suggestions in this book should be used only by golfers in good health. Use common sense, adapt the suggestions to fit your current health concerns, or skip these sections if appropriate. Stop immediately if you experience any pain or discomfort and check with your physician.*

For the putter swing, the relevant body parts to train are your hands, wrists, forearms and eyes. You want to improve your tactile awareness, the functional strength of your hands, wrists and forearms, your eye focus, especially related to your ability to aim your putter and the overall assimilation of your eye-hand coordination as it relates to putting.

Hand squeezes: Squeeze a racquet ball or tennis ball while you are sitting and watching television. Perform an equal number of compressions with each hand. You can also use a hand gripper designed specifically for this exercise, but a ball has the advantage of allowing you to isolate a compression with individual finger and your thumb. Perform squeezes for a total of five or ten minutes with each hand switching hands occasionally.

Basketball Dribbling: Practice dribbling a basketball at different heights off of the ground and with both hands while walking or sitting. In a stationary position, increase the speed of the bounces by dribbling the ball at or less than 12 inches off of the ground. Focus on dribbling with your fingertips and wrists, not the palms of your hands. Your forearm muscles will naturally be activated in this exercise. Repeat with both hands for a period of three to five minutes.

Card Handling: Shuffle and deal cards from a deck of cards. Focus on your finger dexterity and the increase in flexibility this exercise creates in your wrists and forearms. Practice for three to five minutes.

Play Table Tennis or Ping Pong: Rally back and forth with a friend or family member and play regulation games. Try to watch the ball intently on both sides of the net throughout the rallies and try to see the ball hit your racquet/paddle. Keep the ball in play as long as possible and move your feet actively to keep your upper body balanced directly over your hips (center of gravity) and legs. The level of your head should remain fairly constant and not go up or down excessively—try to stay on balance and focus on improving your eye-hand coordination while playing. Also, for fun play a few minutes with your non-dominant hand in order to activate different muscles and to coordinate the exercise of both sides of your body and mind.

Throw Darts: Practice playing traditional dart games. Throw at different distances from the target and occasionally use your non-dominant hand to throw some darts. Focus your eyes on a specific spot on the board during each toss. Follow through with your wrist and forearm finishing pointed at the specific target. Of course, hold the dart with your fingertips and release the dart with a smooth release.

Drawing, Painting, Typing and Handwriting: Work on your fine motor hand skills by doing one or more of these activities. Practice a little with both hands but primarily use your dominant hand. As with any activity, the more your practice the skill, the better you will become at doing it. A good time to draw or practice your handwriting is while you are watching television and a fun activity is to practice signing your autograph in a variety of ways.

Part Two: Specialty Shots and Swings

The Art of Golf involves learning how to play and mastering the execution of a variety of unusual shots you will encounter while playing a round of golf. Oftentimes, you are confronted with situations that require imagination, creativity and a high degree of skill in which to extricate yourself and keep a good round going in a positive direction. Most of these specialty shots are swings that occur near the putting surface and require vision, touch and feel, but there are also several other full swing instances that require extra thought and unique execution. Whenever you find yourself spending extra time analyzing an upcoming shot and its variety of options, you should realize the situation is forcing you to tap into your creativity to select the appropriate club and technique required to hit the shot effectively.

Chapter 6 Bunker Play

General: A bunker is defined in *The Rules of Golf* as a hazard, therefore requiring specific manners of play. The two main things to remember are the following guidelines when playing a shot from a bunker: first, you are not allowed to ground your club in the bunker, and, second, you are not permitted to move any stones, sticks or leaves (loose impediments). If a rake interferes with your ball or shot, there is a different procedure to follow that provides relief from the rake (moveable obstructions). Once you learn how to play greenside bunker shots, you will find it relatively easy to extricate yourself from these hazards with a relatively high degree of success.

Greenside Bunkers

Club Selection: When you walk into a bunker, try to feel the depth and thickness of the sand in that particular bunker. Use your standard sand wedge, the one with 54-56 degrees of loft and 10-14 degrees of bounce for the vast majority of these shots. If the sand is thick and/or soft, which you can also verify when you set your feet into your final stance, you will need to make a swing that approaches the ball from a shallower path that takes advantage of the club's bounce design and removes a fairly large swatch of sand along with the ball. This shallower path, or change in the angle in which your club descends into the impact zone, requires a more rounded or flatter backswing and forward swing. Conversely, if you sense with your feet that the sand is thin and/or firm, your swing should have a steeper, more vertically descending path into the sand so the club's leading edge enters the sand more directly, cutting a divot of sand under the ball. The swing path for this type of shot requires you to take a taller posture in your address position and swing the club on a more upright plane.

The only time to use a wedge with more loft than your standard sand wedge is when a situation requires you to get the ball into the air very quickly (perhaps to fly over an elevated lip of a bunker) and/or the hole location is so close to the edge of the green near the bunker that you need to hit a very short shot with a great deal of spin so the ball stops quickly after landing on the putting surface.

On the other hand, if you are playing a shot from a greenside bunker with the pin on the opposite side of the green or far away from the bunker, and you need the ball to run or roll out to the hole location, you have two options: first, you can stick with your standard sand wedge and close the toe end of the club to a less open position. Then select a spot about an inch behind the ball where you want the club to enter the sand and remove a smaller divot of sand under the ball (that it is resting on because the club doesn't actually touch the ball). Make sure you follow through with your upper body and club and allow your hands to turn-over/roll and release the club after impact with the sand.

Second, you can play the more traditional bunker shot simply using a stronger lofted club such as a pitching wedge or nine iron again with the leading edge of club almost square to the target. This time select a spot one to two inches behind the ball for the club to enter the sand and after impact allow your hands to roll and release the clubhead toward the hole location. The stronger lofted club will cause the ball to fly further than your traditional sand wedge and the ball should roll-out more after it lands on the green. Experiment with these unique situations that occur when playing from greenside bunkers, and develop your ability to select different clubs for these shots and then execute a shot that produces your desired outcome.

Fundamentals: There are several important concepts related to your address position when playing shots from greenside bunkers including the following points:

- your weight distribution should be right-centered at a 55%-45% ratio;
- submerge or dig your feet into the sand about one inch down by *wiggling* them in a back and forth manner that displaces sand and lowers your body;

- the body lines (feet, knees, hips and shoulders) of your stance open, wide to the right and aiming at a spot anywhere from six to ten feet right of your ball target;
- the club face of your sand wedge is laid open to the left but with the center of the leading edge and the face aimed directly at the ball target;
- choke-up on the club an equal amount that your feet went down in the sand, usually an inch;
- your grip is neutral or slightly weak because you will not rotate the club through the impact zone on these shots;
- the shaft is in a neutral or straight position without forward lean in order to activate the bounce of the wedge at impact;
- knees are flexed and your upper body is bent forward at a comfortable angle usually for a slightly flatter wedge swing that cuts into the sand from a shallow path; and
- ball position is approximately one ball right of center or inside the lead foot's instep by a few inches.

Greenside bunker stance and fundamentals

Swing Basics: Obviously, your sand wedge is not allowed to be grounded in the bunker, so start with the club elevated an inch or so above the sand. Start the club back with the rotation of your chest and shoulders with your upper arms connected to the sides of your ribs. Set your wrists very early in the backswing into a fully cocked or 90 degree position, hopefully by the time your hands reach waist height. Rotate only as far as you need to for the distance the shot must fly, usually something short of a full swing or approximately 2/3 of your full swing. Focus on a spot in the sand about two inches behind the ball as your contact area for the club to enter the sand.

Swing the club along your body lines for these bunker shots, slicing across the ball area from outside to inside path in a left to right direction. Greenside bunker shots are unique in that your hands will *not rotate* or turn over through the impact zone. Your trail hand stays underneath the lead hand through the hitting area, and the palm of your trail hand points to the sky throughout the forward swing and follow through. The face of the club remains in an upward position for the entire swing and follow through. The goal is to remove five or six inches of sand that the ball is resting on—two inches from behind the ball and four inches in front of the ball.

On these shots, your club never actually touches or makes contact with the ball; the ball *rides* out of the bunker on the sand your club removes from beneath the ball. Always continue the acceleration of the clubhead through the impact zone. The resistance of the sand is surprisingly strong and will have a significant effect on the club's progress, so think of *accelerating* through the sand. If the shot is of a short distance, take an abbreviated backswing and shorten your follow through, but maintain adequate speed at the bottom of the swing arc when the club enters and cuts through the sand. You might also choose to make a normal sized swing but with less speed and force. This is a more difficult/advanced shot but even if you select this option as the best way to play a shot, you should still make sure the club is accelerating as it enters the sand. Try to *splash* the sand and ball out of greenside bunkers. Some players think of "thumping" the sand with the bounce edge of the sole as an appropriate manner in which to enter the sand with the club.

98

Practice/Drills: Work on an early wrist set by repeatedly practicing the initial section of the backswing. Also, practice the impact zone of the swing in a bunker without hitting a ball, but by removing a six inch swatch of sand. This *divot* should be angled to the right of your ball target. Closely watch the spot in the sand that you want the club to hit first when entering the sand—perhaps mark that spot by placing a tee a few inches from the spot and then checking your divot after the swing to see if you were able to enter the sand at the same point that you had marked with the tee. Practice this impact zone strike of the sand many times and make sure to remove the correct amount of sand that will lift the ball out of the bunker—not too little or too much sand. Try swings of different lengths and of different speeds to see which work best for you in various situations.

Move around in the practice bunker resetting your feet, checking sand depths/firmness and rehearsing the appropriate angle of attack for your swing path to enter the sand. Practice hitting shots to hole locations of different yardages. Hit three shots from one area in the bunker at three different targets, and then move to another part of the bunker and repeat three shots again to unique targets, each time making the necessary adjustment in your stance and swing fundamentals. Look for challenging spots to practice unique shots from the bunker such as a high lip to carry, an uneven/awkward stance or a washed out area of the bunker that has less sand.

Fairway Bunkers

General: Shots that you are forced to play from bunkers that are farther from the green require somewhat different fundamentals and swing basics. These are relatively uncommon shots, and most playing professionals consider the shots from fairway bunkers of 25-70 yards to be among the most difficult shots in golf.

Fairway Bunkers Close to the Green (25-100 yards)

Club Selection: The clubs you use to play these bunker shots should have at least an average amount of bounce (eight to twelve degrees) in order to prevent excessive digging of the club into the sand. The purpose of bounce is to keep the sole or bottom of the club from continuing in a downward path by resisting the sand by *bouncing* the club level, allowing it to continue its *forward* momentum through the impact zone of the swing as long as there is sufficient speed. Shots of these distances are tricky and require feel, touch, finesse, and precision in order to control the ball to your desired distance. Sand will reduce the force of the club coming into impact, so always select a club strong enough to fly the ball the yardage you are facing, plus ten yards. In other words, if you have an 85 yard shot from a fairway bunker and that is the same maximum distance you hit your usual sand wedge from a turf lie, then use the club you carry with the next stronger loft, either a gap or pitching wedge.

Fundamentals: The concepts and fundamentals related to stance, alignment and other pre-swing positions differ slightly for these shots:

- your weight balance remains in the 60%-40% right-centered position;
- work your feet into the sand only far enough to provide stable footwork for the shot;
- square your body into a traditional parallel right alignment position with your feet, knees, hips and shoulders all on the same aiming line approximately three to five yards right of your ball target line, depending on the overall length of the shot;
- the goal for impact related to these shots should be to strike the ball first and then take a small *divot* of sand after the hit—this is the best way to control the distance of the shot;
- choke-up on the grip of the club by an inch so you can "pick" the ball off the sand;
- your club face is square (perpendicular) to your ball target line;
- the ball position is centered or slightly forward of center in your stance between your feet;
- your overall address position is the same as a wedge or short iron shot—knees flexed to achieve the proper height and depth of the swing arc into the shot; and

- your upper body comfortably tilted forward at the hips with a straight spine in order to execute the necessary rotation of the chest and shoulders in the swing.

Your lower body is *inactive and quiet* during these shots, only serving as a stabilizer for your upper body.

Swing Basics: If your feet *dug* into the sand when you took your stance, choke-up on the club an equal amount; you would rather hit this shot a little *thin*, removing little if any sand, rather than hitting the shot *heavy/fat* where you remove too much sand, severely reducing the force at impact and causing the shot to land short of your target. The divot of sand for fairway bunkers, therefore, is very small compared to the divot of sand you take from greenside bunkers. Any distance that suggests less than a full swing will require touch and feel. Control the distance of the shot by either shortening the length of your swing or by reducing your swing speed, although with either option, remember the club should be accelerating and moving at its fastest speed through the impact zone.

Start the club in motion with your chest rotation away from the ball and maintain a light connection of your upper arms and chest. The wrist set is more gradual but should be completed by the end of your backswing, regardless of the length of the backswing. The transition into the forward swing begins with a smooth rotation of the lead hip backwards away from the ball and your head should not move laterally or vertically—maintain a steady spine angle to hold your head position constant during the swing. Rotate through the shot remembering that the rotation of the upper body is generating most of your swing effort. A light grip is recommended in order to *feel and control* the club on partial yardage shots, whereas full swing shots should be made with your normal grip. The swing keys are to strike the ball first, take a small divot of sand and rotate the upper body on both sides of the ball to control the swing length and speed required for each individual shot.

Practice/Drills: Find a practice facility that has a fairway bunker from which you can practice. Work on the techniques and concepts described in this section by hitting eight to ten shots to various targets that are different distances away beginning at 20-25 yards and finishing at 100 yards. Trust your hands and body to learn the best techniques for hitting shots of different distances through your practice sessions. Also, experiment with all of your wedges, including your pitching wedge.

Keep your spine angle and head very level during these swings and try to pick the ball relatively cleanly off the sand with a small divot after the strike. Your swing speed and force should be at about 75% of its maximum to promote correct balance and ball impact, so you should use a club with stronger loft that enables you to make a controlled swing. Your balance will be compromised because of the sand, so a smooth tempo is required to achieve a proper sequence of the large and small muscles during the swing that results in an accurate shot. Stick a tee in the sand opposite the ball so that you can verify the point in which the club entered the sand (hopefully contacting the ball first) and the depth and length of the divot of sand. Repeat 8-10 shots to one target; then hit the same number of shots to a different target 15-20 yards further than the first target.

Continue to practice hitting shots to targets of various lengths focusing on the fundamentals for these swings. Pay close attention to the quality of your strikes of the ball and your ability to control the distances of the shots to your targets. The more time you spend practicing these shots, the better you will be able to see and feel the differences between the bounces and lofts of your wedges, the effect of those club designs on distance and trajectory and the different interaction each has with the sand.

Fairway Bunkers Further From the Green (125 + yards)

Club Selection: Based on the usual distances you hit your irons and hybrid clubs, select one stronger lofted club than you would normally hit for a particular yardage when playing from a true fairway bunker. In other words if you have a fairway bunker shot of 150 yard and you normally hit your seven iron 150 yards, then select a six iron for this shot. You will always choke-up on the club for fairway bunker shots which reduces your distance by at least five yards. Moreover, your lower body will not be as active when making a swing from a bunker which also reduces the *carry* distance of the ball. The combination of these two factors makes the selection of at least one stronger club necessary.

The only other situations you must consider in your club selection for these shots relate to the ball's lie in the bunker, any restrictions or unusual features of your stance for a shot and if there is a feature of the bunker, such as a lip or face, that must be factored into your decision. If any of these issues are relevant and limit you playing a standard fairway bunker shot, then use your regular sand wedge and hit a shot that insures you getting the ball successfully out of the bunker. If possible, consider the remaining yardage of the hole, and try to hit the sand wedge shot a specific distance or to a spot that gives you both a good lie for the next shot and a yardage that you feel confident you can play somewhat close to the hole. The primary goal, however, is to get the ball out of the fairway bunker with one shot.

Fundamentals: Work your feet into the sand about one inch deep and choke-up on the grip of the club the same amount. Take a square iron stance with a 60%-40% weight distribution on your lead leg and foot. Align your body lines (feet, knees, hips and shoulders) to a spot five to ten yards parallel right of your ball target, in the same way that you would for a typical approach shot. Pick a specific object or feature on the course such as a tree or an edge of a bunker to align your body lines toward. The ball position for a fairway bunker shot is the dead center of your stance or slightly back of center. Maintain a natural knee flex for stability and balance and generate the majority of force and speed necessary for the shot through your upper body rotation.

Swing Basics: The club is hovering above the sand; start the club in motion with a smooth and easy rotation of the chest and shoulder into the backswing. Set your wrists naturally during this part of the swing and complete the wrist set by the transition point. Your right arm should remain straight and locked at the elbow joint and the connection between your upper arms and chest should be intact throughout the swing. Maintain a constant height of your upper body by keeping your spine angle and head steady and quiet. Initiate the forward swing with a backward rotation of the lead hip away from the ball. Try to *pick* the ball cleanly off the sand with little or no divot of sand. Rotate your upper body fully in the backswing, change the club's direction smoothly from the transition point and gradually accelerate the club in the forward swing so it is moving at its fastest speed immediately after impact with the ball. Pay special attention to finish your rotation completely into a final follow through position with your belt buckle facing directly at your target. A correct follow through usually ensures acceleration of the club through the sand and overall balance in the swing.

Practice/Drills: Follow the information and recommendations in this chapter and practice, practice, practice. Hit five shots with a variety of your irons and hybrids at specific targets of different distances. Move your practice balls around to different parts of the fairway bunker that demand changes in your stance and set-up position. Also experiment with shots close to a lip of the bunker so you can determine how quickly and to what extent different lofted clubs will elevate the trajectory of the ball after impact when you are faced with that situation.

Your swing keys are striking the ball first with solid or even thin impact, controlling the distance of the shot with the adjustments to your pre-swing and in-swing details and hitting the shots with acceptable accuracy—within five yards to one side or the other of your ball target line. Try to work on these shots one out of every three or four practice sessions. If you can practice 30-60 shots from a fairway bunker each week of the season, you will be ready when this challenge occurs during a competitive round of golf.

Chapter 7 Chip Shots

General: Chip shots are usually played near the green by hitting a short, low shot that rolls on the green more than it flies in the air. Another common name for these types of shots is *the bump and run* which accurately describes a player's strategy for the shot. The usual plan for these shots is 1/3 of the shot's total distance flying in the air and 2/3 of the shot rolling on the putting surface. For many decades this concept has been the preferred way of getting the ball consistently close to the hole. Most professionals agree that the correct play is to get the ball on the ground and rolling as quickly as possible for the best results regarding both accuracy and distance control.

Club Selection: Close to the green, you should select an 8 iron most of the time to play your chip shots. By choosing one club to use for these shots, over time you will develop a feel for the length of swing required to hit the ball different distances in the air and gauge the resulting amount of roll so you will have an instinctive grasp and feel for different shots. Of course, you can use different clubs to play chip shots, but this strategy will require different calculations for the expected ratio of air and roll yardage based on each club.

This is one of *the arts of golf*—determining the correct shot to play, selecting the proper club that fits the shot and executing the fundamentals and techniques required to play the shot successfully.

The total distance a shot must travel in order to finish close to the hole is a key variable when considering club selection. Again, most of the time, try to use an 8 iron, but if the hole is more than 50 or 60 feet away, drop down to a seven iron and apply the same 1/3 air and 2/3 roll formula. To extend the example even further, if you are 20-40 yards off the putting surface with a clear path, you might even select a six iron to run the ball initially through fairway grass and then onto the green and rolling up to the hole location. These are somewhat unusual occurrences but you will find the same shot technique can easily be applied with great success to these longer chip shot situations. Any time that the hole location changes your air/roll calculation away from the 1/3 air, 2/3 roll configuration, say to a 1/2 air and 1/2 roll ratio, then your club selection should change to a club with more loft such as your sand wedge. When this occurs, you are now playing a *pitch shot* rather than a *chip shot*; the pitch shot will be articulated in the next chapter.

Fundamentals: Your stance for chip shots should be with your feet narrow (8-12 inches apart) and your posture upright and tall. Balance your weight right-centered with a 60%-40% distribution ratio on the lead foot and leg. Depending on the length of the shot (and swing) your feet might only be six to eight inches apart on very short shots or spread to as much as 12-14 inches apart for longer chip shots; your feet should be only wide enough to provide stability and balance required for each swing. The stance is open— the lead shoe three or four inches back from the trail foot; your toe line alignment is much further to the right of parallel than it would be on other full swings.

Stance and ball position for chip shots

The swing is so short that the open stance helps promote the proper, natural rotation of the hips and upper body toward the target in the rather short forward swing.

Stand tall with little spine angle tilt and your arms should hang comfortably down from your shoulders with your hands only a few inches away from your belt buckle. Your other body lines (knees, hips and shoulders) are also open at about 10-15 degrees right of the ball target (flagstick or hole) again to assist with an unencumbered rotation of the big muscles as the club impacts the ball. Your right arm is straight and the elbow joint is firm yet your grip pressure is light and the grip position is neutral. You should employ a slight knee flex and slight arch in your lower back; both of these fundamentals help maintain a constant height during the chip which is very important to achieve solid and correct impact with the ball. Your clubface's leading edge is aimed directly at the hole/target.

Swing Basics: As in putting, proper energy transfer from the club to the ball is vital for successful accuracy and distance control on chip shots. Try to hit the ball in the center of the club face or sweet spot.

Look at a specific dimple or mark on the top, back and center of the ball. The swing requires little if any lower body involvement; the feet and legs fulfill the roll of supporting the upper body's balance and height during the swing, and your head should not move side to side or up and down during the swing. Your weight is balanced 60%-40% on the lead leg and foot and is centered in the middle of your feet, under your shoe laces. Extend your trail arm by pressing it down so your lead arm and the club are working together as one unit. This might require you to choke-up slightly on the grip so the clubhead *bottoms out* at the correct height to impact the ball crisply at the low point of the swing's arc.

Rotate your chest back keeping your upper arms connected with your rig cage. Allow the weight of the clubhead to *gather or stop for a split second* at the end of the backswing. Start the club into the forward swing from the transition point by rotating the lead hip and chest together into the impact zone. Avoid the common tendency for the dominant hand to start the club forward and control the rest of the swing by *hitting* at the ball. On these shots there should not be any hinging or unhinging of the wrists during the swing. The clubhead should not pass the hands after impact. Pinch the ball slightly into the ground at impact to impart proper energy and spin into the ball. Think of the club's path as mostly swinging straight back away from the ball on the target line and then straight back down the ball target line at the hole. Your arm connection will actually make the clubhead open on the backswing and close in the follow through similar to a *swinging gate* putter swing. The leading edge of the club must return to the ball with precision so the contact is crisp and solid and under the equator of the back of the ball. Finish your follow through by rotating the hips and chest through and past the impact zone and ending at the target.

Practice/Drills: Scatter ten balls in a six foot area two to five feet off the surface of a practice green in various lengths of grass and with different lies. (This area is the 12 o'clock position for your practice session.) Using an eight iron, hit those chip shots to a specific target on the practice green. Move to another area about ¼ of the way around the green (say the 3 o'clock position) and repeat the drill. Now move again to the 6 o'clock position of the practice green and repeat the drill, again challenging yourself to hit 10 different shots from 10 different situations (short grass, long grass, buried lie, etc.). Finally, move one more time and repeat the drill for the last time from the 9 o'clock area around the practice green.

The four separate spots should have provided you unique practice scenarios from many angles, distances and lies so you are ready for the constant variety of greenside chip shots you will encounter while playing on a course. Pay keen attention to proper impact and the key fundamentals while practicing these finesse shots around the green.

Next, select a practice area approximately 20 yards from the front edge of the practice green. Again scatter ten balls in a six foot area and using a seven iron, chip shots through the cut grass, similar to a fairway, that flies about 1/3 or the total distance of the shot and then rolls the final 2/3 or the yardage to the target. Pick a spot on the grass about 1/3 of the way as the landing point for the shot. A dark or light patch of grass is usually available for the aiming point. Then repeat the drill with a six iron. These longer chip shots will require a wider stance and a slightly longer swing, but your fundamentals and swing basics remain unchanged. This experimentation will give you a good idea how easy it is to play these kinds of chip shots.

Practice short chip shots where the ball is off the putting surface but on the tightly mown grass of the fringe/collar of the green or the fairway and the hole location is relatively close to the edge of the green. Use an eight iron and hit a few shots. If the ball goes too far with this club, even with a very short swing, you should use a different option.

The best option is to simply use your putter and hit a putt through the combinations of short grasses. Practice rolling putts through different lengths of longer cut grass to develop a feel for how much the ball is slowed down and how to best gauge the overall swing length required to reach the target using this option. Your putter is typically a very accurate way of playing these shots but distance control is predicated on your ability to sense the proper swing based on your instinctive touch, feel and finesse.

A second option for playing these types of shots is to use a putter swing while hitting the ball with a hybrid club. The hybrid's loft will lift the ball into the air for a short distance over the longer grass and then allow it to roll the remaining distance with accuracy. Some players are able to control this *hybrid putt* very well after some practice because of the unique advantages of the weight and mass built into the design of a hybrid club. Of course, you will need to choke-up significantly on the grip of the hybrid club and take a stance more similar to a chip shot than a putt. However, use a putting swing or stroke. Experiment with these different techniques and clubs, and you will increase the number of options you have in your repertoire for dealing with tricky shots around the green and improving your scores.

Chapter 8 Pitch Shots

General: When the situation you are presented with near the putting green calls for you to hit a shot that will blend air time and roll time for the ball, say 50% of the total distance in the air and 50% of the total distance rolling, you will play a *pitch* shot. Many players prefer to hit what amounts to pitch shots, using their sand wedge, all of the time near the green, foregoing chip shots from their list of options. The problem with only pitching the ball around the green is that the point of impact has to be more precise with the more lofted club than it when you play a chip shot with a less lofted club, leaving little margin for error in the swing. So, a miss-hit pitch shot will usually have a worse result than an equally miss-hit chip shot, meaning the chip shot is the higher percentage and safer shot and will save strokes on your scorecard over the course of a competitive round. Obviously, a skilled golfer should have the ability and expertise to play either shot and should use good judgment while playing to select the club and shot that is most appropriate for the situation and will produce the best result.

Club Selection: Pitch shots are played exclusively with your wedges. Use your standard sand wedge (54-56 degrees) for 75% of these shots. By using this one club most of the time, you will develop the instinctive feel necessary to play shots from a variety of situations. Pitching the ball is the choice when a shot requires you to carry the ball in the air somewhere between 40%-70% of the total distance in the air and the corresponding 60%-30% of the total distance rolling to the hole. Your sand wedge is versatile enough to play low shots that either roll-out some or spin to a relatively quick stop depending on the technique and nuance you employ when playing the shot. Moreover, your sand wedge is very effective playing shots out of the rough or heavy grass and likewise can be used from short, tightly mown grass with equal delicacy and precision.

The 25% of the time when you need to switch to a different wedge is somewhat self-evident and dependent on the specific circumstances of a shot. Use a less lofted wedge (your gap or pitching wedge) when the situation calls for an imbalance of less air and more roll, say 40% of the total yardage in the air and 60% on the ground, or when an even 50% air and 50% roll shot that you want to make sure rolls enough, for instance to a green with an uphill slope to the hole location. On the other hand, you should select your lob wedge (58-62 degrees) when the imbalance between a shot's carry and roll percentages are reversed, say 75%-90% of the total distance in the air with only a minimal amount of roll. Even more extreme versions of these specialty shots will be discussed in more detail in an upcoming chapter, *Lob and Flop Shots*. The choice of playing pitch shots near the green with your pitching, gap and lob wedges will not occur very often, but you should be well versed in the use of these clubs for such exacting shots when the situation arises.

Fundamentals: Most of the concepts and fundamentals for hitting pitch shots are very similar to those of chip shots with a few exceptions. Typically, pitch shots will be played from distances that require a more athletic stance, longer dynamic swings and increased body involvement. As you know, your wedges are the shortest clubs in your bag so your spine tilt should be slightly more forward from the hips and your knee flex should be slightly deeper than with chip shots. The stance, however, is similar—your feet are relatively close together 8-16 inches apart depending on the length of the swing and your lead shoe is several inches back from the trail foot and open to the target.

Your other body lines (knees, hips and shoulders) should follow your toe alignment. Overall you stance will be open approximately 10-20 degrees parallel right of your ball target. The longer the pitch shot, the wider your stance and the bigger the swing. Also, on longer, fuller swings reduce the openness of your stance squaring your body lines closer to the ball target line.

At address have your right to left weight distribution a full 60% on your lead leg and foot and your feet should be balanced evenly with the static weight of your body on the center of each foot under your shoe laces. The ball position for pitch shots is centered between your feet for a 50% air and 50% roll shot. Adjust the ball position forward of center toward your lead foot for more loft and air time or conversely, slightly further back toward the trail foot for less carry and more roll on the shot. Your hands are close to your hips and pressed slightly forward to promote a descending swing path and crisp impact with the ball before hitting the turf. The right arm is straight and rigid, again working in concert with the club as a single, long unit that swings from the lead shoulder and when playing these shots using a small amount of wrist hinging. A slight arch in your lower back and level hips will assist you in maintaining your spine angle tilt and overall height during the swing.

Swing Basics: The pitch shot is basically a partial or half swing— sometimes a little more and sometimes a little less. The difficulty lies therein. It is easier to control a short chip shot swing or a full shot swing than it is to maintain the balance and precision required to make a pitch shot swing. Your center of gravity is in your hips and mid-section and one key for returning the clubhead to the ball at the proper point or bottom of the swing arc is to make sure your *hips are level* at the end of your pre-swing position. In order to achieve a neutral or level hip position you might have to deepen the flex in your trail knee slightly more than your lead knee because of your body's tilt onto the lead side. The swing is controlled by the rotation of your chest. Your upper arms are connected to the chest and you should have a small amount wrist or hand action, unless you are at an awkward distance that requires a 3/4 length swing, such as 40-60 yards.

The wrists will be more active when pitching the ball from further distances to the hole and when playing from lies such as thick rough that require more clubhead acceleration to execute the shot. Your stance should be open to help with the rotation in the forward swing and follow through, but make sure it doesn't hinder your backswing by shortening it—if this happens, simply square your stance slightly so you can make a proper rotation on both sides of the ball. Maintain a level head with no up or down movement and also restrict any lateral movement left or right of your spine, hips, chest, neck and head. Rotate the upper body smoothly and gracefully providing the required power into the shot by the length and speed or your core rotation. Your hands and the small muscles of the wrists and forearms provide your connection to the club and give you feel during the shot, but try to keep their involvement primarily for control, not for power or energy. Accelerate the club through the impact zone, as always, and complete the rotation of your chest and hips finishing with your belt buckle facing the target and on balance.

Practice/Drills: Take a proper stance for a pitch shot and practice gently brushing the top of the grass with slow and even 1/2 swings. Verify your ability to bottom-out the club and the lowest point of the swing arc by hitting a spot in the grass or by clipping the top of a tee you stuck in the ground. Experiment with different lengths and types of grass and from different types of lies. Make longer swings feeling the rotation of the body and stillness of the head. Think of hitting the pitch shot with your chest rather than your arms and hands; they are just your connection to the club and should remain passive unless the shot calls for a high degree of touch and finesse.

Scatter balls in a variety of areas and distances around a chipping/practice green. Practice with your usual sand wedge for most of the session experimenting with the variety of shots you can produce with this one club. Pick a landing spot for each shot so you learn to control the carry distance and match the length and speed of the swing to your desired amount of air time for the ball. Change the ball position back in your stance and experiment in the same manner testing the unique ball flight trajectories and corresponding spin rates you can produce by de-lofting the club and hitting down on the ball.

Use your different wedges and monitor the effects each of these clubs produces on high and low shots, spin and roll-out shots and which combination of club and technique produces the best results. Select different targets to hit shots toward and vary your target often, so you challenge yourself to practice a variety of shots and increase your skills and options for competitive play.

On the practice teeing area, you should warm-up by hitting 1/2 shots with your wedges. Pick a spot 30 yards from you and hit three or four shots to that target. Increase the distance by ten yards and hit a few more shots. Continue to increase the distance and change targets in ten yard increments until you are hitting to a target 60-75 yards away. Your swing will progressively lengthen and become more dynamically athletic at the same time that you are building a subconscious feeling for the swing lengths and speeds necessary to hit shots to the various distances.

Add more wrist set for longer pitch shots

Less than full swings, or in-between shots, require weekly practice. Let your hands and muscle memory system control the distance of a partial shot, and trust your core muscles to make a repeatable swing that produces accurate shots. A *quiet* lower body and head will help you make consistent, solid contact with the ball, which is of paramount importance on short shots in order to control the accuracy and distance of the shot.

Chapter 9 Lob and Flop Shots

General: The most delicate, precise and *surgical* swings are required to hit effective lob and flop shots. These are short shots near the green that you want to play with the *most carry or air time* and the *least amount of roll*. When well executed, they are shots of extraordinary finesse and skill, but the choice comes with risk.

What makes lob and flop shots so risky is the small margin of error that occurs at impact; contact between the club and ball must be almost perfect. The bottom of the swing arc must reach its lowest point immediately following impact and the leading edge of your lob wedge must be at exactly the correct angle and height when this part of the wedge slides under the back of the ball.

Any deviation from near perfection will result in a mishit shot that leaves you at best in a similar position or at worst with a much more tenuous situation for your next shot. On the other hand, the lob wedge is a unique club that can sometimes extricate you from nearly impossible predicaments if the shot is played properly with touch and skill.

Club Selection: Always use a lob wedge for these high, soft shots. The stated effective loft of the club is measured when you have the club shaft straight in line with your arms and the leading edge of the club face is square to your target. The loft of the club can be manipulated, however, in one of two ways. A forward press of your hands slightly in front of the ball will cause the shaft to lean with the grip ahead of the clubhead causing the club to lose a few degrees of loft. If you couple this adjustment with a change in ball position—moving the ball further back toward your trail foot—you will de-loft the club even more.

On the other hand, more loft can be added to your lob wedge by opening the club face behind the ball (the toe of the club opens away from the target line); this additional loft can be exaggerated by a change in ball position to the right of center closer to your lead foot. Also, couple this change in ball position with your hands being even with clubhead and virtually no shaft lean in your set-up position. In other words, the shaft is straight and the end of the club is pointed at the mid-section of your body. Using one of the adjustments will change the loft by approximately two degrees and if you make both adjustments, the result will be a change of approximately three to five degrees in effective loft for the shot you are about to play.

Fundamentals: Your grip should be soft/light and you should grip the club with the hands in a neutral position. The stance is slightly open to the target for partial/half swings. Full swings with your lob wedge will most often be played with a square stance with body alignment lines aimed at a parallel right target. The lob wedge is a very short club so your knee flex is deep and your spine tilt should only be as far as needed to sole the club evenly on the ground, so the toe is neither down with the heel up or vice versa with the heel too far down and the toe up off the ground. Your footwork for lob and flop shots is minimal—feet stay flat on the ground with little or no rolling of the feet inside your shoes. Your trail foot heel will come off the ground near the finish of your swing during the follow through.

Maintain the connection between your upper arms and your chest but relax your arms because most of the time, these shots need to be played with more arm, wrist and hand action to promote touch and feel in your grip. The core muscle of the upper body will, of course, rotate to provide the energy for the swing, but your small muscles must be highly sensitive and activated in order to control the clubhead through the impact zone.

During these swings it is imperative for your head to remain as still as possible and for your spine tilt to remain unchanged. Make your eyes focus intently on a dimple or mark on the top, back and center of the ball in order to give your eye-hand coordination the best chance to return the club to the ball for precise, solid and clean contact. The leading edge of the club is square (or perpendicular) to the ball target line on lob shots of any distance.

When hitting a flop shot which maximizes your ball flight and minimized roll, the leading edge and club face should be open and laid back to the target—this will probably cause the leading edge to raise 1/4 to 3/8 of an inch off the ground because of the club's bounce. Use the bounce of the club to help the clubhead slide under and past the ball rather than digging into the turf and stopping. This creates a situation where the bottom of the swing arc must return to the ball with absolute precision in order to pinch exactly in the narrow space between the back of the ball and the turf. Flop shots should only be played when the lie is *fluffy* and the ball is *sitting-up* on the grass enough for the leading edge of the club to slide/slice easily under the ball. If the ball is sitting down or the lie is very firm, simply abandon the flop shot and play a lob shot that you can execute effectively.

Swing Basics: The rarest quality of these two shots is that they should be hit with a more equal combination of the small muscles of the arms, wrists and hands and the big muscles of the hips, chest and shoulders than any other shots in golf.

During these swings, your lower body is very passive and quiet, only serving to stabilize the upper body, spine and head. The upper body rotates as much as is needed to hit a shot of a particular distance but your arms should lag slightly behind the rotation of the core muscles and gently *swing* the club into and through the impact zone. With lobs, your wrists will set 90 degrees into a fully cocked position and your hands will rotate or turn over during impact releasing the club. The opposite hand action is required for flop shots—your hands should *not* rotate or turn over. As in greenside bunker shots, flop shots call for your dominant hand to stay underneath the top hand of your grip during and after impact without rotating. If this is done properly, the palm of your dominant hand will point up to the sky and the face of the club will point up to the sky during the forward swing and into the final follow through position. Watch the golf ball intently, focusing on a tight spot or dimple on the top of the ball, until it disappears after impact.

The clubhead should always accelerate through the impact zone and work past your hands immediately after striking the ball. Rotate your upper body as far forward into the follow through as you rotated in the opposite direction during the backswing—a rotation of equal length on both sides of the ball.

Practice/Drills

One Arm Swings: Right arm only swings will help you establish the swing basics for lob shots. Start with short, 1/2 swings with the right hand holding the grip of the club in the usual spot. Hit soft pitch shots using only the right arm and hand to control the club.

Progressively make longer swings engaging the big muscles of the chest and shoulders to help generate more speed and force through an upper body rotation. Maintain a straight, firm right arm during your swings. Practice hitting a dozen shots using this technique.

Then switch the club to the left hand and make left arm only swings repeating the drill. Allow the left hand to rotate or turn over during these progressively longer swings. As with the right arm swings, work hard at minimizing unnecessary body movement and maintaining control of the club. Try to hit these practice shots solidly on the center of the club face.

Switch the club back to the right hand and arm and repeat the drill starting with small, soft swings but this time *do not* rotate or turn over the hand and wrist; for these swings the right palm should point down at the ground during impact and the follow through.

This is the proper hand action for flop shots, so in this segment of the one arm drill you are practicing the different hand and wrist action required to differentiate and play the two types of shots with your lob wedge. Hit a dozen balls and then switch the club back to your left hand and arm. Begin with small, soft swings and again do not rotate or turn over the left hand and wrist. Hold the palm up to the sky position through the forward swing and follow through to learn the proper left hand action for flop shots. Again hit a dozen shots using this technique.

Two Arm Lob Shot Practice: Start at 25-30 yards and progressively hit a handful of shots at targets about five yards further from each other until you reach 60 a distance of yards. Pay close attention to your distance control of these shots. Increase the yardages of the shots by gradually increasing both the speed and length of your swings in subtle increments. Hit three or four shots from 25, 30, 35, 40, 45, 50, 55 and 60 yards from tight lies of closely mown grass. Then repeat the yardages hitting a few balls the same distances only this time from the heavier, longer grass of the rough.

Two Arm Flop Shot Practice: These shots are typically played from shorter yardages such as 5-25 yards from the flagstick. The ball's lie must be *sitting-up* on the grass leaving enough room under the ball for the club to easily slide under it through the impact zone. Hit three or four flop shots from a variety of lies including both shorter and longer cuts of grass and from different distances to targets on the practice green.

Work around the green hitting shots from areas around the full circumference of the green so that you are challenged to practice flop shots from many unique situations. The swing should be long and full for these shots and remember to accelerate the club through the impact zone in order to achieve the proper height and spin on these shots. Practice both lob shots and flop shots several times a week so that you reduce the risk of these shots and can play them comfortably when situations arise during a round.

Chapter 10 Other Shots

Every player encounters a myriad of unique situations while playing golf that require special knowledge and talents to deal with effectively. In this chapter we will discuss the following occasional, yet in some ways common challenges we face on the course:

Uneven Lies; The Rough; Escaping From Trouble; ShapingShots; and Playing in the Wind and Rain.

Uneven Lies: Most golfers realize there is a cause and effect relationship regarding ball flight when the ball is resting on a different level or plane than the golfer's feet. The following causal relationships are the rule of thumb:

• Side hill lie: ball above your feet—the ball will curve left to right

• Side hill lie: ball below your feet—the ball will curve right to left

• Uphill lie: left foot lower than right foot—the ball will fly straight or left to right

• Downhill lie: right foot lower than left foot—the ball will fly straight or right to left

Uneven lies require you to play a balanced, well struck shot in spite of the changes inherit in your stance and address position. Select one stronger lofted club than the yardage would suggest so that you can make a swing at 75%-80% of your maximum swing speed and maintain your dynamic balance. Uphill lies might even require selecting a club of two stronger lofts because the ball's trajectory will be higher than usual which also shortens the overall carry distance of the shot. On all four of these shots, your ability to create a stable stance will be challenged. This might require more or less spine tilt, more or less knee flex and/or an unusual, uneven angle for your hips and shoulders depending on the lie. On uphill or downhill lies, try to match your shoulders and hips to the slope so all three are parallel with each other and make a swing that follows the angle of the slope. A shot played from an uphill lie will have a higher trajectory and will not roll out much after it lands on the ground whereas the opposite is true for a shot played from a downhill lie.

One early decision you must make for each of these lies is whether to play the natural curve of the shot that the lie will cause, or to make an attempt to negate that natural spin by adjusting your grip and/or swing mechanics. Unless a hazard or object necessitates the latter option, you should simply align yourself further to the right or left of the normal parallel right body alignment target and make your usual swing allowing the natural curve parameters described in the chart at the beginning of this chapter to affect the ball's flight. Your power source for all of these swings should be your upper body core muscles. The lower body must function more as a stable base for your upper body rotation, which again should be a little less forceful because of the stronger lofted club and your slower, more controlled swing. This should assist you in maintaining your overall balance and help your eye-hand coordination return the club to the ball correctly thereby increasing your likelihood of making solid impact in the center of the club face.

An important principle to follow on uphill and downhill lies is to set the angle of your hips and shoulders parallel to the angle of the slope of the ground. Once you have established your stance for the shot, your goal should be to swing the club holding your address position constant so that the bottom of the swing arc occurs properly through the impact zone. The club should make contact with the turf and remove a divot without digging excessively into the ground or the arc of the swing *bottoming-out* without touching the ground.

When you are faced with an uneven lie, find a spot near the ball with the same slope characteristics and make several practice swings in order to gain a feel for the adjustments you must make for the upcoming swing. Pay careful attention to your stance and your ability to keep the club moving through the swing at an effort level or speed that allows you to maintain your dynamic balance, strike the ball solidly with a reduced swing speed and complete your follow through rotating fully at your target.

The Rough: Obviously, no two lies or shots in golf are exactly the same, which is one of the most difficult and challenging aspects of the game. Every lie in the rough is unique, but generally speaking, clubs with more loft will play more effectively from the rough than straighter faced clubs, especially irons. Whenever possible, try to hit the ball with no grass, or as little as possible, coming between the ball and the club face. Your stance is 60%-40% right-centered with more of your static weight on the lead leg and foot and the ball position should be approximately 1/2 ball back from the center of your stance than it would typically be for the club you are playing.

Lift and hold the club at the top of the grass. This will allow your initial take-away of the club in the backswing to be unencumbered and untwisted by the rough. Choke-up slightly on the grip of the club and select a club with one stronger loft than the yardage typically requires; the heavy grass will usually slow down the club's acceleration as it passes through the impact zone and/or cause an imperfect hit off the center of the club face. The stronger lofted club should counteract those variables and make the ball end up at your desired distance for the shot.

Hitting shots from the rough requires strength and clubhead speed. Take a slightly stronger grip than usual, about 1/2 inch further to the left for these shots, so your hands will rotate or turn over in spite of the resistance of the rough. Your swing effort and speed should be greater than usual; about 90% of your maximum level, as long as your stance is good enough to support a swing of that speed. Rotate the upper body and shoulders in a full backswing to the transition point, because the extra speed of the swing should come from a fully loaded core and a straight, tight right arm. As always, make a smooth transition that is initiated with the rotation of the lead hip back and away from the ball, not a sliding forward with the hip. Sliding toward the target with the lead hip is a common tendency most golfers have when hitting shots from the rough; the upper body and hip slides to the right in what feels like a way to generate more power into the shot.

Rather, you should keep the hips, arms and club rotating together in conjunction with the chest to gather increasing, unified speed coming into the impact zone. Your forearms, wrists and hands will turn-over and release the club creating maximum speed and energy transfer at the point of impact between the club face and ball. The swing path should have been more descending or steeper than usual attempting to contact the ball first or with as little grass as possible between the club face and the ball at impact. Maintain the upper body's rotation to the right and fully into the follow through position on shots from the rough.

If you are faced with a long shot from the rough, use a hybrid club; the mass and weight of the club's design allow it to move effectively through the rough without the likelihood of the club turning, either into a more open or more closed position the way a long iron is likely to do as it encounters the high grass entering the impact zone.

The strongest lofted iron you should attempt to play from the rough (of course, depending on the thickness of the grass) is a six or possibly a five iron. A six iron or any of your irons with more loft have the ability to cut the rough effectively, but if the distance of a shot requires a club *stronger* than a six iron, use a hybrid club and either choke-up on the grip to reduce the distance of the shot or shorten your backswing and forward swing to accomplish the desired yardage. Whenever one of these full swing options does not appear to be viable, select your standard sand wedge and simply use the techniques describe above to advance the ball safely into the fairway at a distance from which you have a chance to hit a good shot into the green and possibly save par or drop no more than one shot on the hole.

Escaping From Trouble: Inevitably you will hit shots while playing that result in difficult situations from which to play your next shot. First of all, as a side note, realize that hitting an escape shot is one of the simple symmetries between golf and life. Everything doesn't go always go as planned in golf or in life, and we demonstrate our strength of character, moral fortitude and reasonableness when we are faced by obstacles and problems to overcome. So, the obvious lesson is to keep this in mind and maintain self-control and a proper perspective when you find yourself in a tough spot on the course.

Your mind should work in two ways: initially, view the situation with the determination to get yourself out of trouble in as few shots as possible—hopefully with only one swing; and secondly, take a few minutes to assess all of your options, from the safest to the riskiest, from heroic to cowardly and everything in between while quickly weighing the percentages for success and the ramifications of escalating problems related to your options.

Most of the time, select the safest shot that will get you out of the woods or high grass immediately and with one shot. Moreover, select the club that gives you the greatest likelihood of playing the shot with success. For some reason, our instincts almost always start at the end of the spectrum of choices with the highest degree of risk, contemplating the shot options with the greatest chance of failure, and more often than not, we determine the gamble as worth taking in spite of the overwhelming odds against playing the shot successfully.

Rather, try to think logically and conservatively when a bad swing puts your ball in trouble on the course. Then spend the remainder of your time going through the preparatory decisions and fundamentals required to play the shot. Unless your lie dictates something extraordinary, choose a club that fits the easiest escape shot—the chip shot, or punch-out back to the fairway with a six or seven iron, is usually one of the safest and best options. You know there is a built-in margin of error with chip shot swings and the corresponding clubs that improves your chances for success.

The next best escape shot option is usually a pitch shot with a wedge. Again depending on the situation, your sand wedge is your all-purpose, go-to club that can advance the ball from almost any lie as long as you pay careful attention to the fundamentals of the pitch shot and execute a clean strike on the ball. Partial swings or half swings are the next best option for escaping from trouble, but avoid compounding the initial difficulty by trying to regain too much, too quickly. This usually occurs if you try to advance the ball too far toward the green while also attempting to remove the ball from trouble, such as hitting a shot out of the woods through a narrow opening between two trees 40 yards ahead of us while keeping the ball beneath a low canopy of tree limbs with the ball sitting on a bare lie with no grass and a tree root a few inches ahead of the ball…don't laugh, we've all done it too many times. When you find yourself contemplating the nearly impossible rescue shot, think about life—be smart, be safe and use your mind and skills wisely to overcome adversity as quickly and effectively as possible.

Shaping Shots: Today's golf balls and clubs are designed and constructed with materials meant to hit the ball with a straight trajectory. However, it is hard for a golfer to repeat a swing that produces a consistent straight ball flight. That being said, you have natural swing characteristics that produce spin on the ball in the same way most of the time. Your swing routinely produces *straight spin* (backspin or over spin) or *sidespin* in either a left to right or right to left direction. Work to hone your swing fundamentals to the best of your physical ability and then stick with your natural ball-flight spin tendencies, unless you make a conscious decision to curve a particular shot with a specific shape to match the hole.

If possible learn how to shape a shot with a slight fade, with subtle right to left side spin, and build your swing around those fundamentals, because it is easier to control the amount of spin on the ball with a small degree of right to left spin. Your hands will *rotate or fire more slowly* on a fade than on a draw swing, so a resulting out of control slice is less likely than a badly hooked shot if your timing gets out of sync in a particular swing. Also, this shot shape generally does not roll-out as much as a shot with the opposite side spin which adds another layer of overall control to a fade or cut shot.

Obviously, if you can hit straight shots most of the time, you will post low scores and play the game at a high level. Regardless of your preference, it is important to understand your swing traits well enough that you can shape shots in both directions whenever it is necessary.

There are three ways to shape shots: first, you can simply change your grip which slows or quickens the rate and speed that your hands rotate the club through the impact zone; second, you can adjust your stance more open or closed which changes the path of the club as it passes through the impact zone; or third, you can alter the timing and synchronization of your swing.

Changing your grip is the simplest technique you can use to impart spin on a shot. In order to curve the ball from right to left and hit a fade, you should weaken your grip by moving one or both of your hands further to the right on the grip of the club. Your thumbs should end up on the top of the shaft when you look down at them. This grip change slows down your hand rotation at the bottom of the swing arc so the club face is slightly open when it contacts the ball, producing right to left side spin. Conversely, in order to create left to right side spin on the ball, adjust your hands to a stronger grip position by moving one or both of your hands further to the left by an inch or so. This adjustment creates very fast wrist and hand rotation through the impact zone, turning the club face in a closed position at impact, which creates the desired left to right side spin. Experiment initially by adjusting only one hand for some practice shots and then hit additional shots after you have changed your grip with both hands.

You should witness different and exaggerated results between the two adjustments. For some golfers, a grip change alone will be sufficient to change the flight of the ball, but for others, more is required.

If you need to make a second adjustment to shape the ball, try making a change in your stance/set-up position. For a fade, open your stance by moving your lead foot two or three inches back from a square toe alignment with the trail foot. For a draw, do the opposite. Close your stance by moving your trail foot back two or three inches back from a square toe alignment with the lead foot. Start with minor adjustments and progress to more dramatic changes until you achieve the correct combination that results in your desired ball flight. Accompany the change in your toe lines with a corresponding change in the lines of your knees, hips and shoulders, so all four of these alignment lines are in unison with one another. So your four body lines are all either open together or closed together, not just your feet.

Occasionally a player finds it easier to maintain his/her normal grip and stance and instead, make a swing adjustment as a technique to create side spin on the ball and change its trajectory. For a fade, the club needs to be moving on a path slightly from outside the ball target line to inside and across the ball target line while traveling through the impact zone to impart right to left side spin on the ball. For a draw, the opposite must happen—the club impacts the ball while traveling on a path through the impact zone from slightly inside the ball target line to the outside of the ball target line which imparts left to right side spin on the ball. This option for shaping shots requires a player to change his/her swing plane slightly in order to accomplish one of these two impact positions. The plane for the fade starts with the club moving more upright and outside the normal path during the swing and the plane for the draw calls for a flatter and more inside club path and swing.

The same effect can also be created by un-syncing your arms and body from working together with a unified timing sequence during the swing. For a fade, let the timing of your body get slightly ahead of your arms as they move in the forward swing. Your arms should lag slightly behind your body entering the impact zone which creates a slower speed and rotation of the club, leaving the face a little open when it contacts the ball. For a draw, the arms race slightly ahead of the body which creates a closed clubface at impact, imparting left-to-right spin on the ball if timed correctly. In both of these options, you are deliberately not returning the club to the ball with a square club face, and you are purposefully disconnecting your body and arms from working together in delivering the club back to the ball. This option works best for advanced players and is counterintuitive to most of the principles and concepts that are recommended in this book.

Shaping shots through grip changes, adjustments in your stance/set-up or minor alterations in your swing path/plane are the safer and more reliable options for curving the ball and shaping shots to fit course conditions.

Occasionally, you will encounter situations on the course that require you to hit a shot with more or less height than your typical trajectory. The simplest way to alter your ball flight height is to change your ball position. To hit the ball higher, move the ball forward in your stance toward the lead foot and center the weight distribution of your stance to a 50%-50% position between your two feet. Also, your hands, arms and the club should be in one line behind the ball with little or no forward lean to the club's shaft. Your stance should be slightly more upright and the plane of the swing should follow accordingly. Slow the rotation of the club face by taking a slightly weaker grip and try to shape the shot as a fade.

For a ball flight that is lower than usual, move the ball position further back in your stance toward your trail foot and assume a right to left weight distribution to at least 60%-40% or even 65%-35% onto the right side—hip, leg and foot bearing the bulk of your static weight. Your stance should be slightly closed with a deeper knee flex and more spine tilt. Take a stronger grip to accelerate the rotation of your forearms, wrists and hands through the impact position. The desired swing path is a little flatter and these adjustments should produce the left to right shot shape or a low draw.

Spend some time during your practice sessions shaping the ball from left to right, right to left as well as with high and low trajectories so you are ready for any challenge on the course. Also, these are advanced skills, and as you increase your ability to hit the ball in different ways, you will also increase your control of the ball and become a better *ball striker.*

Playing in the Wind and Rain: Nothing fights the effects of wind and/or rain on a golf ball more than hitting the ball solidly in the center of the club face. Touring professionals will deliberately slow down the speed of their swings and reduce the force and effort of their swings in order to hit the ball solidly when playing in difficult weather conditions. A well struck shot in the middle of the club face produces optimal energy transfer from the club to the ball. A shot that hits the sweet spot of the club face flies farther and on a tighter/straighter line than an off-center hit because the transfer of energy is flawless. So, it becomes imperative to repeat these types of swings as often as possible when playing in the wind and the rain.

Driving the ball in tough weather conditions requires patience and discipline. Dry the club face and grip one final time before you take your stance. Tighten and shorten every aspect of your fundamentals and swing. Narrow your stance slightly and spread your toes inside your shoes so you feel like you are *gripping* the ground with your feet before and during the swing—it should make you feel like you have a very solid connection with the ground. Your feet should remain flat on the turf until the final approach into the impact zone when the trail foot pushes down gently during the bottom of the swing arc and then rises onto the toes in the follow through.

Your weight distribution should be balanced on the lead leg and foot at a 60%-40% or a 55%-45% ratio throughout the swing. Overall, your stance and posture should be upright and tall. Your knees should have a relaxed flex throughout the swing in order to preserve your spine angle tilt. Try to keep your head from moving side to side or up and down. Let the core muscles of your hips and torso swing the club and maintain a strong upper arm connection with your chest. Correct synchronization and sequence during these swings is of the utmost importance. Focus your eyes on a dimple or mark on the ball during the swing until the ball disappears following impact. Reduce your swing speed and effort to approximately 75-80% or your maximum capacity in order to maintain your dynamic balance and produce a swing with smooth and efficient timing. Finish your follow through completely on your right side with your chest facing the target.

Playing iron shots in the wind and rain also requires you to shorten and tighten your swing; this promotes crisp, solid contact between the club and ball. Your stance/set-up fundamentals are the same as for driver swings—60%-40% weight distribution on the lead side; toes spread and feet flat on the ground; and a relaxed but purposeful knee flex to anchor and brace your upper body during the swing.

The ball position for iron shots should be 1/2 inch or one inch further back in your stance from the usual ball position, toward the trail foot. Choke-up slightly on the club and select a club with one stronger loft than you would normally select for the given yardage.

Strengthen your grip by about 1/2 inch to the left, and open your stance a small amount—lead foot about one inch back from your square alignment line. Follow your standard iron swing fundamentals and concepts other than shortening the length of your backswing to increase your control of the club. The forward swing is naturally more descending into the impact zone because of the change in ball position. Just make sure to continue the acceleration of the clubhead during the forward swing and impact with the ball. Finish the rotation of the upper body in the follow through with the chest facing the target. The ball flight or trajectory should be lower than normal, and the ball should bore through the wind and rain in a piercing manner.

The five elements for playing effective shots in inclement weather are the following keys:

1. choke up on the grip and make a slower, more controlled swing;
2. watch the ball intently until it disappears after impact;
3. make solid contact with the ball in the center of the club face;
4. accelerate the club through the impact zone; and
5. complete your upper body rotation into a balanced follow through position.

Value the accuracy of your shots over the distance of the shots when the weather conditions are challenging. Finally, maintaining a positive attitude and a patient perspective will help you post your best score against your fellow competitors, who are also experiencing the ordeal of playing golf in the wind and the rain.

Part Three: Miscellaneous Topics

Most of the game of golf consists of making a series of full swings and partial swings to hit shots from an endless variety of situations. Your skills and decision-making abilities are under constant scrutiny as the game forces you to change from dynamically charged, powerful swings to subtle chip shots and putter swings that require precision and deft touch. But there is more to the game—much more.

In this section, we will cover a variety of topics that relate to practicing with a purpose and playing the game with a maximum level of control and adroitness. Once you truly embrace the difficulties and challenges of golf, you will find that one of the major goals you will list every year that you play is to determine what areas of your game are most in need of improvement. Next you will need to develop a strategy and plan of action to address the areas of your game you target for improvement, and finally create a way to assess your progress.

The chapters in this section may only appear to relate tangentially to playing better golf, but they are all necessary parts of the whole— managing your mind, your nerves and your physical body in order to play your best golf. Some of you, especially accomplished and experienced golfers, might find that the areas of your game with the greatest need for improvement are found in one or more of these related, miscellaneous topics. Perhaps a refinement or subtle change in your pre-shot routine or the way you practice in preparation for playing competitive rounds of golf will have as much of an impact on your ability to score than will adjustments to one of your swings. Regardless, there is always something new to learn about golf, and we can all continue to amass a broader base of knowledge to draw upon while we strive and work to become better players.

Chapter 11 Pre-Shot Routines

We all have pre-shot routines—some are better than others. We use them before every shot whether we realize it or not. Being creatures of habit, we brush our teeth and put on our shoes virtually in the same manner each day. Our everyday routines in life are *subconscious* habits, and unfortunately, we typically use the same approach before we play a golf shot. A more effective behavior prior to making a swing is to follow a conscious framework, or deliberate pre-shot routine, in which we organize our thoughts before we start the club in motion. This is a better method for two reasons:

first, your pre-shot routine should create a sequential structure and hierarchy for your options so you can quickly and effectively make decisions that will produce a positive result; and,

second, the process should relax your mind so that you maintain a calm and even pace, pull your attention into the present moment and focus your attention on the task at hand instead of outside distractions.

A rehearsed and positive pre-shot routine coordinates our mind and body to perform a specific task which increases the likelihood of success. There are two parts to a conscious and effective pre-shot routine.

The first part is simply the selection phase. Each time we approach a shot we have options and choices. Your thought process is engaged in making decisions related to issues such as your yardage for the next shot, the unique characteristics of the lie, the type of shot to play and the club to use for that shot. The second part of the process is the important sequence and framework of thoughts related to the execution of the swing that you should consider prior to putting the club in motion. This structure should include the following five elements that will be shot specific:

1. proper parallel right alignment of your body lines at a target;
2. visualization of the ball's flight, trajectory and landing area;
3. the rehearsal of a slow, smooth practice swing;
4. eyes focused on a spot or dimple of the ball to enhance your eye-hand coordination; and
5. one key swing thought to have foremost in your mind while the club is in motion during the swing.

These items represent a checklist of sorts that should be performed in the same order prior to every swing.

Stand directly behind the ball on the ball target line for the first three steps of this routine and perform the steps with the following thoroughness:

- firstly, select the aiming spot/target parallel right of the ball target, approximately three to ten yards depending on the length of the shot, for the alignment your body lines;
- secondly, while standing in the same spot look at the ball target and visualize the ball's flight, shape and trajectory for the shot you intend to play; and
- thirdly, again from behind the ball, make a controlled, slow practice swing that would produce the shot you just visualized.

This practice swing also serves to loosen your muscles and joints for the upcoming movement and it should also imprint the muscle-memory of the swing you have visualized for the next swing in your system. Some players prefer two practice swings, which is fine as long as you are consistent with your routine.

The last two parts of your pre-shot routine occur after you take your address position. Take your stance paying particularly close attention to aiming your body lines at the parallel right target that you previously established and then settle into your final stance. Next focus your eyes on a specific spot, dimple or mark on the ball and maintain that visual throughout the swing. Finally, think about your one key swing thought you want to have for the swing; for example, maintaining the flex in your trail knee or starting your forward swing with a short slide and smooth rotation of your lead hip.

All in all, this may seem rather involved but when you think about the items, you already do many of these steps out of necessity or just by habit—the problem is you might skip some important thoughts or replace them with other extraneous ones. Once you develop a positive, structured pre-shot routine, it will become an efficient framework in which to organize the precious time before you play a shot. This routine should be used before every shot you play, even short shots and putts.

For competitive players who play tournaments, leagues or games among friends, a purposeful pre-shot routine will help you deal with the pressure of competition and keep nerves somewhat under control. Consider adding a breathing component to your pre-shot routine when you play competitive rounds. Taking and expelling a deep breath is a proven way to regain composure mentally and physically before making a swing. Lose yourself in the process, and then try to execute the shot to the best of your ability.

While practicing on the range, also practice and work through your pre-shot routine in order to commit it to memory and make it an instinctive process. Not only will you have a specific goal in mind for each shot, but it will also serve to slow you down between shots while you are practicing, which, of course, mirrors the timing of playing a round of golf. Too often on the driving range we mindlessly hit ball after ball very quickly focused more on the physical aspects of the swing. When we play golf, there are often several minutes between shots and your mind is engaged in many decisions regarding your next shot and the corresponding fundamentals you must employ to execute the shot. Practice your pre-shot routine while hitting balls on the range in order to better train your mind and body to work together and your scores will improve.

Chapter 12 Common Rules and Golf Etiquette

The Rules of Golf consist of 34 different rules—each containing many sub-sections—several appendixes, and numerous definitions that apply to the interpretations of the rules. Most golfers concede that knowing every rule comprehensively and knowing how to correctly interpret and proceed under the rule in every situation is nearly impossible. The rules are so complex and open to different interpretations that the United States Golf Association (USGA) actually prints a dense book of *Decisions* regarding the rules that is many hundreds of pages in length. So, don't feel alone if you do not view yourself as particularly well versed on the rules of golf—it is common, even among experienced golfers. This chapter contains a brief review of the most common rules and options that frequently occur while playing, as well as, advice on appropriate behavior and etiquette that you should know and follow when playing golf with others.

General: Before starting a round there are three things you should do and discuss with your friends, opponents and/or fellow competitors. First of all, each player should mark his/her golf ball in an individual, unique way with a marker so it can be identified on the golf course if necessary. Show the other players your mark, the brand and type of ball you are playing and the number on the ball.

Moreover, mark a second ball that is different in some way from the first ball, such as a different number, type of ball or your individual marking, and have that ball in your pocket so it is readily available if you have to play a provisional shot without having to take the time to go to your golf bag, find a different ball and mark it. If the situation arises that you need to play a provisional shot, simply pull out the extra ball from your pocket and announce to the other players that you plan to play a provisional shot. Show and/or tell the other players in your group the identifying characteristics of this ball which should be different in some way from the first ball. Also, if you switch balls during a round, you should announce this ball change to your playing partners and reveal the new ball's identifying characteristics to them before putting that ball in play.

The second thing you should do before you start your round is to discuss with the other players if the group is *playing the ball down* on the course in the upcoming round or if an adjustment to this foundational rule has been made by the players or governing person(s) because of the course conditions, for example, lift, clean and place or *winter rules*.

The last item to discuss before the round with your playing partners is to decide how to handle *order of play* for the round. There are two systems: 1. *the honor system* on the tee, where the player with the lowest score plays first; and the *honor system* also suggests that the order of play on the course will be determined by distance from the hole location—the person furthest from the hole is next to play; or 2. *ready golf* which is a random order of play based on the readiness of each player—obviously, the players still take turns, but whoever is ready can address their ball and play their shot.

Discussing these questions before the round begins establishes the basic ground rules, levels the playing field for competition and clarifies the courtesy and procedures for play.

Etiquette: There are countless elements and issues regarding golf etiquette that players will learn over many years of playing the game, but the following list is common behaviors that everyone should abide by during play.

Pace of play: Play the game at a brisk pace, without undue delay and always have the goal to stay in contact with the group of golfers immediately in front of you on the golf course. If that group is slow and a gap of one hole or more exists between them and the group in front of them, golf etiquette suggests that they should allow your group to *play through*. Avoid over-analyzing your shots, making too many rehearsal swings or other habits that slow down the progress of your group such as marking the players' scores while parked near the green instead of pulling ahead to the next tee and then marking the scorecard.

Where to stand or park your cart: If you are near another about to play a shot, stand or park at least ten feet to the front side of the person, so the player can simply look-up and see where you are— not behind the player or in back of him/her which can create a safety concern and/or distract the player visually or mentally. Whenever possible, stand or park far enough away from other players so that you are very clear of them, as much as 10-20 yards away. Similarly, on the teeing surface, stand to the front side of the player, as far away as possible, so the person hitting a shot does not feel *crowded* in any way. On or near the putting surface, stand far away from other players and far away from the hole. Do not stand behind a player; do not stand in a player's sight line or line of putt; do not step on any player's line of putt; and do not cast a shadow near the player or on the player's line of putt.

Be ready to play: Regardless of which option your group is using to deal with the *order of play*, prepare for your upcoming shot as much as possible without distracting others, so that when it is your turn to play your shot, you can proceed without delay. Another aspect of being ready involves moving forward to your ball, or searching and finding your ball, while others are playing their shots; do this only if you can remain safe and stay out of harm's way while moving slightly ahead of them.

Help other players watch their shots: Watch the shots of your playing partners, and try to pick out a tree or another identifying feature on the hole that is in line with the shot or near the spot that you saw the ball land in order to help them easily find their shot when the group progresses on the hole. Find your ball and then, if necessary help others locate their balls, so a player is not searching for his/her ball alone. If everyone in the group helps each other, balls will be located more quickly and the group's pace of play will continue in a positive manner.

Be considerate of others: Use common courtesies both within your group as well as with other groups in your vicinity on the course. Switch your cell phones to vibrate and only take calls of extreme importance. Also, avoid swearing, being loud, or yelling *("go in"* or *"get in the hole")* on the course; experienced golfers find these comments irritating, obnoxious and unnecessary.

Care for the course: Leave the course in better condition than you found it by not only repairing your own divots and pitch marks but by also repairing those problems left by less considerate players. The course should be in the same condition, relatively speaking, for golfers playing after you, and fixing turf problems reduces the cost of maintenance and presumably, greens fees. Moreover, help the grounds crew by picking up cans and litter that might have been dropped or blown out of carts and throw broken tees off the teeing ground to save time and mower repair expense.

Rule Procedures

General: Whenever you are faced with a situation that involves a specific rule, confer and discuss the situation openly with the other player(s). Not only will this clarify the specifics of the rule but also insures that the procedures of the rule are being followed correctly.

If there is uncertainty about a rule or procedure, discuss the situation with the other players and then play two balls out to completion on the hole from that point—the original ball following the rule you think applies to the situation and a second ball from that point without the ruling (or vice versa). For example, if your shot is in an area that might or should be ground under repair but it is not marked as such, you can play the original ball from that spot to completion of the hole and then with a second ball, take a drop at the point of nearest relief from the ground under repair and also play that ball to completion of the hole. You should record both scores and then, after the round, discuss the situation with the golf professional or a staff member of the course for a ruling of which ball is indeed the correct ruling and correct score.

Markings: Many courses don't have the resources to continually stake out-of-bounds lines and hazards and mark areas that should be identified as ground under repair. Or sometimes the paint marking those areas has not been refreshed or the painted area has been cut but is still somewhat visible. If you are ever in a situation where you are not sure if your ball is in a hazard or an area of ground under repair, call over at least one of the other players in your group for a discussion and a decision regarding the situation.

Provisional ball: Anytime you hit a shot that might have landed out of bounds, in a hazard or into an area that might result in a lost ball, play a provisional shot before walking to the area of the original shot in case when you get there the ball is indeed, out of bounds, in a hazard or lost. Announce your intention to your playing partners, show them the details and markings of your provisional ball and hit that shot after all of the other players have played their original shot.

You are not obligated to play the rest of the hole with the provisional if your first ball is found and is in play, but hitting the provisional shot speeds up play in the long run. Suggest this procedure to other players during your round who hit shots that also might be out of bounds, in a hazard, or have the potential to become lost balls.

Nearest point of relief: The nearest point of relief is defined as the closest point on the course to where the ball lies and then a drop within one club length of that spot. For example, your ball finishes on the center of a cart path. As a left handed player, your nearest point of relief will be on the right side of the path, not the left side.

This is the case because it might only be 30-36 inches to the right of the ball's position on the path for the ball to be clear and away from the path. Whereas to the left of the cart path there would be the same 30-36 inches for the ball plus an additional 40-50 inches for the player to make a stance that is not touching the path, making a total of 70-100 inches for the player and the ball from the original point if the ball is moved to the left of the path. So, the 30-36 inches to the left of the original spot on the cart path is the nearest point of relief.

Taking a drop: The procedure for taking a proper drop is to stand erect with your arm straight out at shoulder height and drop the ball. The ball must stay within the one or two club lengths (depending on the reason for the drop) of the nearest point of relief and no closer/nearer to the hole. The player should have marked the acceptable drop area with a tee at each end of a club prior to making the drop.

If the ball rolls out of the drop area or closer to the hole, the player should follow the same procedure and re-drop the ball. This time if the ball does not stay in the appropriate drop area or rolls closer to the hole, the player should place the ball on the spot where the ball hit the ground on the second drop.

One club length or two club lengths? If you are getting relief from a situation *without a penalty*, you are entitled to a drop area within *one club length* from the nearest point of relief. On the other hand, if you are *incurring a penalty stroke*, you are entitled to a drop area within *two club lengths* of the nearest point of relief.

The Five Most Common Rules

Lost Ball: (Rules 24-28 for various situations regarding lost balls) A ball is lost if it is not found and identified by a player within five minutes after a search has begun for the ball. If the player has played a provisional ball, that second ball now becomes the ball in play under penalty of stroke and distance (if the lost ball was a tee shot, the provisional ball has a score of three strokes); or the player must return to the spot where the stroke was played that resulted in the lost ball and play a new ball under penalty of stroke and distance. There are exceptions to this rule that are covered in other rules—for example, if the ball is in a man-made obstruction or in a water hazard, a different procedure may be chosen to follow.

Out of Bounds: (Rules 27, 20 and 13) The area beyond the course boundary, marked by white stakes constitutes out of bounds. The ball must lie completely beyond the line marking the boundary to be out of bounds and if the ball is on the line, the ball is in play. If a player's ball is out of bounds, the player must return and play another ball from the spot from which the original ball was last played under penalty of one stroke. In other words, if a player's tee shot is out of bounds, the player returns to the teeing ground and plays a second ball with his/her third stroke on that hole.

Water Hazard: (Rules 26, 25, 24, 14 and 12) Any sea, lake, pond, river, ditch, surface drainage ditch or other open water on the course should be identified as a water hazard. These hazards are marked by yellow stakes. *Lateral* water hazards that are located parallel with a hole are marked by red stakes. The ball may be

146

played from a water hazard without penalty; or under penalty of one stroke, a ball may be played from where the last shot was played; or also under penalty of one stroke, a ball may be dropped any distance behind the water hazard keeping a straight line between the hole and the point where the ball crossed the margin of the hazard. For lateral water hazards, the ball may be played from the hazard without penalty; or under penalty of one stroke, a player may drop a ball within two club lengths of the spot the ball crossed the margin of the hazard or on a line between the hole and the point the ball crossed the hazard on the other side of the water hazard.

Ball Unplayable: (Rule 28) Other than from a water hazard, elsewhere on the course if a player believes his/her ball is unplayable, under penalty of one stroke, the player may choose from one of the following three options: 1. play a ball from where the last shot was played; 2. drop a ball any distance behind the point of where the ball lay and a straight line to the hole; or 3. drop a ball within two club lengths in any direction of where the ball lies, not nearer the hole.

Wrong Ball: (Rules 15, 30 and 31) A wrong ball is any ball other than the player's ball in play or a provisional ball. A player who plays a wrong ball incurs a penalty of two strokes and must correct his/her mistake by playing the correct ball or proceeding under the applicable rule.

Unlike any other game, golf is played on thousands of *unique playing fields*, and there is not a set of standard court or field measurements or boundaries. When most of us play golf, there are no umpires or officials on the course to insure that the rules are being followed and that correct scores are being recorded. Golf courses exist in mountains, deserts and plains in every part of the world. Accordingly, The *Rules of Golf* have been written and revised every four years so they are flexible and can be interpreted and applied in a manner that is fluid enough for the appropriate decisions to be rendered based on the specifics of the particular situation; always with fairness to the players. The spirit of the game implies that golfers should work cooperatively within the context of the common rules and exhibit sportsmanship and competitive honesty while enjoying the challenges of the game and the friendships we acquire and cherish over the years with other golfers. Serious and tournament golfers should own a copy of *The Rules of Golf,* and read through them periodically in order to stay familiar with the related issues and procedures that govern the proper playing of the game.

Chapter 13 Scoring and Course Management

Playing golf for a score is the purest form of the game, and perhaps the most challenging. It is a rare day indeed that a player hits the ball into every fairway, onto every green and holes out in two putts, the way par was abstractly conceived and constructed. As in life, a round of golf will inevitably throw unexpected challenges at you, try your patience and test your will power and self-discipline. Golf forces you to deal with unforeseen and unwanted turmoil during a round and your success or failure depends on how you manage your thinking, emotions and abilities in the face of these obstacles.

Simply put, scoring means getting the ball into the hole in as few strokes as possible eighteen times. Par is the benchmark all golfers judge their performance against. An analysis of shots played during a typical 18 hole round of golf reveals that a player putts the ball 25-40 times, probably 1/3-1/2 of the player's total strokes. A player hits his/her driver an average 10-14 times and his/her fairway metals and hybrids five to ten times. Iron shots make up 15-25 shots and the remaining 5-15 shots will be played with wedges— some with full swings but many with partial swings. Of course, the actual numbers will vary from one round to another, but the point is players use their scoring clubs most frequently and should base their practice time around these percentages. So if you want to score well, you must putt well, first and foremost.

Practice putting every day, outside or inside, no excuses if you want to post lower scores. The important point is to build your confidence so that you can roll a ball on the exact line you select, or at a specific spot such as a coin, from short distances, say two to four feet. Playing professionals practice five to eight foot putts endlessly, because they know if they can make a high percentage of these putts around the hole they will save par when they miss greens and they will make birdies when they hit great approach shots. In short, their livelihood depends on their ability to make putts within eight feet of the hole consistently.

Unless you are a *great ball striker* who always hits a very high percentage of greens in regulation, the next element of scoring you should spend time practicing is your short game shots near the green. These include chip shots, pitch shots, lob and flop shots and greenside bunker shots. The third area of the game that relates most to scoring are your full swing clubs—irons, hybrids and fairway metals since at least one of these clubs will be used on every hole. Accuracy and distance control with these clubs will not only result in an increase of greens hit in regulation but also shots that end up close to the hole; both of which save strokes.

Finally, practice accuracy with your driver. You must be able to drive the ball accurately to have any chance of posting a good score on a given day. Too often, however, golfers practice with their clubs in the reverse order from which the clubs impact their scores. Commit yourself to a more logical balance of practice time with your most important scoring clubs in order to shoot lower scores.

Course management is another important element of scoring. Three general areas of this concept are worthy of review:

1. playing practice rounds;
2. planning a strategy for play; and
3. knowing how to react and manage a bad situation when things go wrong on the course.

Playing a course before a competitive round has obvious benefits. You are scouting the golf course so think about your strengths and weaknesses as you play the various holes. Play a set of middle tees unless you know already know you will be playing another specific set of tees; for instance college players know they will play from one of the tees furthest back and conversely a group of senior players might always play tees specific to their age group. Buy a yardage book if one is available and mark spots and make notations on each hole. If the course does not sell a yardage book, make good use of a scorecard.

As you play, get a feel for the overall space and length of the course. Find the ideal landing areas for your drives on the par 4s and par 5s and conversely, note areas of the course to avoid. This might include such realizations that hitting a driver is not the best percentage play on a specific hole. Make similar observations about your approach shots; for instance, one side of the green may fall off steeply, making a missed shot that lands there almost impossible to recover from and make par. So make notes about the areas near and surrounding each green. You could simply mark *"no"* in the spots you want to avoid and *"ok"* where a miss still gives you a chance for an up and down. Most greens are built with unique features that you will also want to make note of, such as a ridge or an elevated section.

During a practice round, roll putts not only toward that day's hole location but also in other directions so that you get a feel for speed and slope in several directions. Mark the slope directions of the different areas of the putting green so you have a simple way to confirm your reads during the competitive rounds.

Draw arrows in the direction of the slopes, mark ridge lines and make general notes about any important green characteristics such as overall slope and drainage in your yardage book. Elevation changes and prevailing winds should be noted if you sense either of these features make a difference in club selection. It might be necessary to select a stronger lofted club than the yardage suggests or vice versa because of the topography or wind. Because you are on an *information gathering venture* make as many notes as seem relevant because this information will become the basis for the next phase of your course management, making a plan.

Develop a strategy to use when preparing to play a course that involves matching your strengths and abilities to the course's features. First determine which holes are on the extremes—the easiest holes that provide the best chances for birdies and the most difficult holes where you would be satisfied simply making pars.

Develop both an aggressive strategy for playing the easiest holes and a conservative strategy for playing the hardest holes. Next, methodically review your notes and impressions for each hole in the order you will play them. Create a strategy or play for each shot on each hole, bearing in mind what to avoid and more positively, where to hit each shot.

Approach shots should always start from the center of the green. Know the yardage to the center and have a plan with a clear ball flight line to the center. As you play the course you will need to decide which hole locations are generous enough for you to hit directly at because there is some margin for error and on the other hand, which locations should be played away from because there is little room to miss the shot without bringing a negative situation into play.

A good course set-up will include a mix of *green light, yellow light and red light* hole locations, and you can calculate the best approach shot distance by computing the center of the green yardage factored with the specific hole location and the surrounding risks.

For example, the yardage to the center of the green on a par 3 is 160 yards and the hole location is short, in the front section of the green, maybe 15 yards short of the center of the green. There is a pond in front of the green with a steep wooden wall. Select a club that will play ten yards short of the center distance, or 150 yards, so you build in a margin of error in case your shot is not struck perfectly or in case there is another variable that reduces the distance the ball flies, such as wind or cold temperature. Your goal should always be to avoid or play away from the trouble (a pond, a sand bunker or a deep collection area) on approach shots while still giving yourself a chance to putt for a birdie or to two putt for a par. Advanced players will include their preferred shot shapes while developing their overall strategy on how to best play a golf course. As always, the shots you have confidence in playing should also be a consideration in your planning and overall strategy.

Finally, your plan of attack can only be developed in the abstract and before you actually start the round. It is an initial guide for you to follow to the best of your ability as the best way to start each hole, but the plan will undoubtedly need to be amended while you are playing out holes. The key is to begin each hole according to your pre-determined strategy and to stay focused on executing the plan one hole at a time, regardless of what has already occurred in the round. When things go differently than you had planned, it is becomes vital to think logically, think clearly and most often, think conservatively through your options. Your initial tendency will probably be to envision the *best case scenario* and results for the next shot. Oftentimes, this line of thinking and the selection of the wrong option for the shot, results in a *worst case scenario* and outcome.

Assess the situation on a risk/reward continuum. If a shot has less than a 75% chance of success, choose a more conservative alternative. It is one of the most difficult things to do in golf, but minimizing the damage on a hole to your overall score can turn momentum in your favor again quickly, whereas making a triple bogey or worse can derail a round or tournament score beyond the point of recovery.

If your drive on a given hole misses the fairway, determine the safest path from that point to the green. If you have a 75% chance or greater of making the green with the next shot, then play it. Usually this shot will need to be played to the center, widest part or most open area of the green rather than directly at the flagstick. On the other hand, if your chance of making the green with the next shot has less than a 75% likelihood, determine the most direct path to the hole in two shots. Work backwards from the hole dividing the distance into two shots. Select your desired or favorite yardage for the second shot and then try to execute the first shot (maybe an escape shot) so that it finishes close to the area you want to play the second shot from.

Following a tee shot, if your ball finishes in a position (for example, deep in a wooded area) that prohibits you from making a full swing and approach shot to the green, find your safest path to escape the trouble and get the ball back into the fairway with just one shot. Approach shots played from the fairway should be played to a conservative area of the green off the center of the green and toward the pin location—such as, a back pin position would equal the yardage to the center of the green plus eight yards, etc. Only play approach shots directly at the flagstick when you are able to use a short club that you feel very confident playing, and even then at a spot slightly away from the close edge or short side of the green.

Most of your chip shots will be played directly at the hole. Pay particular attention to distance control as your final thought after you have aligned your body and club for accuracy. The goal of every chip is to finish the hole with no more than two more strokes—the chip shot and one putt, so try to leave your chip shot very close to the hole if it does not go in on its own.

Pitch shots and lob shots might need to be played slightly away from the hole so that you get the ball onto the putting surface for certain, as well as give yourself a chance to save par with your putter.

The best way to approach course management related to scoring is to have the goal of making your *highest* possible score on any hole a five. Moreover, try to play your entire round without hitting a single shot in a hazard or out of bounds. Lastly, no three putt greens! Work hard to leave your lag putts as close to the hole as possible, regardless of the length of the lag putt; your odds of making a putt that is longer that 12-15 feet are very low, so stopping the ball near the hole by employing good distance control should be your highest priority.

Chapter 14 Golf Psychology

How hard can it be to play golf? The ball is sitting perfectly still and the club is large and forgiving. On television, the game looks so easy. But even playing professionals admit that they only hit a few shots *perfectly* in each round. In fact, the best players in the world hit shots out of bounds, into hazards and among the spectators. Some of them score in the 80s at every tournament and miss 18 inch putts; but the players who are not playing at their best that week are not shown on television. So, to paraphrase a famous golf statement—golf is a game of misses, and it's the quality of your misses and your ability to manage your mistakes that determines your score.

It is a fact that playing professionals possess a higher degree of athletic talents and skills than do amateur golfers; professionals often work with instructors and coaches and are very knowledgeable about their swings; professionals have highly tuned, custom fitted golf clubs; and professionals have practiced and played golf far more than average golfers. So, considering all of this and the fact that even they have bad days or spells, then it is important for golfers reading this book to approach their playing of golf both reasonably and realistically.

From a purely physical perspective, it is a certainty that you will *miss* (not strike the ball perfectly in the sweet spot) many, if not most, of your shots during a round. However, mentally, we can be comparable to the best golfers in the world if we use our minds properly. Here are a few random thoughts regarding the psychology of golf.

Positive Attitude: Try to maintain a positive attitude while practicing and playing. Approach each shot during a round with an attitude of low expectation and indifference of the result. Take your time and try to execute each shot within the best of your ability. If you make a bad or flawed swing on the course, get the ball back into the fairway immediately and return to a positive attitude as soon as possible. Next, posting as low a score as you can on that hole should be your immediate goal. The tee shot on each hole is a new beginning—a round of golf has 18 new beginnings if you make sure to treat each separate hole as a new event.

Resiliency: Be as resilient as possible in the face of adversity—the game has a knack for exposing even the most subtle flaws and shortcomings, both physical and mental. You are human and you will make mistakes or not execute swings to perfection. Have the mental resolve to realize you are just as likely to hit a good shot on the next swing as to continue in a negative pattern. Give it your best effort to make a par or birdie as soon as possible after a bad hole in order to reverse a negative trend. Practice your fundamentals on a regular basis and improve both your strengths and weaknesses throughout every season.

Par is your benchmark: Compete with the score of *par* and the challenges of the golf course. Focus your thoughts on your strategy for play and your swing fundamentals; don't get caught-up with what your playing partners are experiencing. During a round, almost everyone will have trials and tribulations to deal with. Try to take care of your own business and work to achieve your personal goals.

Calmness: Maintain a sense of calmness through the ups and downs of your round. Inevitably, good and bad things will happen. An even temperament and a calm demeanor are the best defenses against the emotional highs and lows that you will typically experience while playing. Take deep breaths occasionally and relieve tightness in your body by stretching and shaking out tension in your muscles during the round. Try to do your best on every shot and accept the results as an indication of your humanness.

Composure: What other people think of you as a *person* is much more important than what they think of you as a *golfer*. Always consider your behavior as indicative of your character. Your treatment of others is your legacy—set a high standard for yourself.

Stay in the Moment: Perhaps the most difficult but most important psychological aspect of playing good golf and finishing good rounds with low scores is the ability to keep your mind focused on the present time and events. Discipline your mind to focus on what you are doing right now or in the next few minutes and nothing else. Give your full attention to the next swing and shot. The worst thing you can do is to allow your mind to wander and start thinking about your overall score or some concern in your everyday life. Keep your mind focused on the task immediately in front of you, shot by shot, hole by hole. The end of your round is the time to add up your numbers and tally a score.

Pre-Shot Routine: Concentrate on your pre-shot routine—both parts. Get your yardage, think through shot options and select a club. Select your parallel alignment target and ball target; visualize the shot; take a practice swing or two feeling the shot you want to make; address the ball properly; focus on a dimple and reduce your mind's focus to one *swing thought*—for example, maintain my spine angle tilt and height during the swing. Start the club away from the ball *low and slow* with a rotation of the chest and shoulder and watch the ball disappear.

Commitment: Stick to your game plan and strategy for playing each hole. The work you put in on course management deserves a chance. You conceptualized your plan logically and unemotionally free of the stressors of the round, so give it a chance—play within your strategy at the beginning of each hole. Golf is a *tortoise and the hare* fable only with a ball and clubs—be methodical and patient over the four hours of the tale.

Trust Your Practice: Even touring professionals admit to being nervous and stressed in big moments. Try to relax your muscles and emotions; take a few deep breaths and *shake-out* the tension in your hands, shoulders and neck. Swing smoothly and let the big (core) muscles you've been training do the bulk of the work in a full, balanced swing; and always finish your rotation and follow through at the target.

Visualization: Visualize making every putt from 15 feet or less (while being mindful of distance control as your final thought before moving the putter). *Roll* the ball gently toward a specific spot, either at the apex of the break or near the hole. Remember, this is the artistic and creative part of the game that requires your best touch and feel. Embrace this challenge—it is a highly developed skill. Golf is like life; there are constant and unexpected challenges. Golf is difficult, and it requires patience, strength (both physical and mental) and self-discipline. You don't know what will happen next, in spite of your planning, experience and skill. True wisdom tells us to enjoy our time on the course and the friendships we make playing the game. As in life, always give your best effort and appreciate the opportunity to learn more and constantly improve.

Chapter 15 The Golf Ball

Not all golf balls are created equally. A host of performance variables, construction processes and design features separate the vast array of golf balls available to golfers today. Another complicating factor is the wide span of price points for consumers to weigh while attempting to find a ball that will enhance their shots and elevate their games.

The Rules of Golf specify the size, weight, overall distance, and initial velocity limitations for the modern golf ball so there is a common standard among golfers. Although there has been an ongoing discussion of creating a different set of ball standards for playing professionals, usually in the context of limiting distance, at this point in time, amateurs and professionals play the same golf balls, for all intents and purposes.

Golf balls are x-rayed as a final function at manufacturing plants and sorted into three groupings; balls with the tightest tolerances and smallest imperfections that are sent to the professional tours for use in tournament play; balls within an acceptable range of imperfection for sale to the golfing public; and *irregular* balls that are offered for sale as *X-Outs* because they do not meet the acceptable standards of the manufacturer.

Since the production of balata covered balls with liquid centers and wound rubber cores was discontinued almost two decades ago, all golf balls are now of solid core construction. Despite this commonality, there are many physical characteristics of importance that you should be aware of and research during your quest to find the left golf ball for your game. The first design feature to review is the number of layers there are in a specific golf ball's construction. This number may vary from as low as two layers to as many as seven layers. A ball with only a few layers is typically made of cheaper materials, is less expensive to produce and is marketed as a *low-end, basic* golf ball. On the other hand, a multilayered ball with three or more layers is generally made with several very thin layers of advanced materials over a more expensive core that has been created for a specific playing trait, for example, a firm ball that has the ability to stop rather quickly on the green. These extra layers add steps to the production process and, obviously, this increases the cost of the ball.

Researchers and designers of golf balls continually experiment with several other physical characteristics of the ball in their search for product improvement. The number of dimples and the shape of the dimples affect the spin rate, distance and trajectory a golf ball. Moreover, there are many different patterns in which to arrange the dimples, such as inter-connected diamond or triangle designs, each with purported advantages.

Balls with highly visible covers in enhanced optic colors such as yellow, pink and orange have become popular in recent years. Although manufacturers claim this feature of color does not have an adverse effect on playability as compared to similar types of balls with traditional white covers, most professionals disagree. This opinion has driven balls with colored covers toward the less expensive range of the golf ball spectrum—for beginning and novice golfers because they are easier to visually locate by players who typically hit more errant shots.

The performance characteristics that are the most important to serious golfers are *feel* and *spin rate*. *Feel* is most important in putting. Determine for yourself just how *soft* you like the golf ball to feel when you strike it with your putter. If your putter has a solid steel face, you will probably want a ball with a soft cover and feel. Conversely, if your putter has a soft insert or is made of a softer metal such as aluminum, a ball with a firmer feel might be the right combination for you. Experimenting with the feel you desire with your putter is the first priority. There are balls that feel soft and balls that feel firm throughout the range of moderately priced and expensive golf balls, so do your research. After you decide which type feels best to you with your putter, play some holes with that type of ball on the course. Start with a sleeve of balls from two different manufacturers that are comparably priced at a moderate amount. Verify which ball has the best overall feel for you with all of your clubs and on all shots.

Spin rate is probably the single most important performance variable for you to consider once you are able to hit the ball consistently near the center of the clubface with all of your different clubs. Spin helps you control your shots. Search for a ball that feels good to hit and performs with control on your full and partial swings. Again, conduct technical research about different balls you are considering, especially related to spin rate. Select a ball with the feel you prefer, soft or firm, and then experiment with a sleeve of the most expensive balls offered by two manufacturers. Depending on your swing speed, ball speed off the club face, angle of attack on the forward swing, and launch angle following impact, some balls might actually *spin too much* for you, causing shots to fly too high and/or not fly the distance you expect.

Another caution is that a ball can feel *too soft*, as well. This reduces your touch which is vital for short shots around the green. So, don't think that a ball touting the softest feel or the highest spin rate is necessarily the best ball. Some of this decision is personal preference and some is how the *ball performs* for you and your swings. Also, the most expensive ball is not necessarily the ball that will perform the best for you. Finding the proper blend of feel and spin in your golf ball takes patience and experimentation. Over time, try to find a ball that feels good and performs well with all of your clubs. For most players, the golf ball is the final piece of equipment that pulls together all the external elements of the game and merges them with the player's talents and skills, producing the best chance for scoring.

Chapter 16 Custom Equipment and Technology

Since 2000, the research and development operations of golf equipment companies have made the greatest advancements in equipment since the breakthrough innovations of Karsten Solhiem some fifty years earlier. Virtually every single piece of golf equipment can now be customized to a player, from clubs, to balls and even shoes. Regardless of the skill level, number of years of experience, gender or age, every player can improve his/her game simply by using proper equipment that is customized for that player.

But, how should you proceed on your journey through this morass of information and choices? There are two choices — experiment on your own through *Demo Days* or sample clubs from fitting carts now available at many golf courses. You can purchase different golf balls and shoes and try to match them to your other equipment on your own. Or, you can find a PGA Professional in your area that you trust and whose judgment you have confidence in and who is knowledgeable about today's equipment options.

Start the process by examining your current equipment and determine how it connects with you—your swing and skill level. The second approach will save you time and money in the long run, but some people would rather experiment and make purchases privately. Most likely you will need to do some experimenting on your own with the smaller accessories to build your entire apparel and equipment package regardless of whether you are working with a professional or not.

Before you make equipment changes, begin by taking a lesson and playing a few holes with a professional in your area. You want improvements to occur in both your swing and your equipment, and the equipment changes you make should be harmonious with the improvements and changes you are making in your golf swing. Because of current marketing strategies, club manufacturers would like to see you every club separately. So, the trick is to customize all of your 14 clubs even if you purchase them at different intervals while at the same time connecting them together effectively to form a holistic unit that complements and maximizes *your game* going forward into future seasons. This process is sometimes more art than science; even touring professionals are careful and methodical about making these kinds of adjustments and they have the advantage of working directly with the R & D experts and technicians when auditioning and considering new equipment. Most professionals use the off-season to test and make equipment changes so they have ample time to become accustomed to the new clubs prior to the beginning of their new competitive season.

Oftentimes, the final settings to your adjustable clubs will be the last step of customization. Obviously, the settings can be changed to match your swing changes when they take hold and become more physically engrained and repeatable.

Your professional will help you develop a buying plan that includes piecing together a proper sequence of clubs in your bag as well as unifying the look, feel and performance characteristics of the equipment. The individual parts will make sense when you put them together and perform well as a whole entity. This should be accomplished by blending data from two sources. The first source is technological information from launch monitors such as ball speed, clubhead speed, launch angle, carry distance, angle of attack and others. Moreover, computer analysis of your swing using video taken during your lesson(s) will help you and your professional connect the necessary adjustments in your golf swing and options in new equipment. The second source of data is less empirical and more subjective—the way the club feels to you as well as the objective feedback of the ball flight, distance and trajectory each club produces during your practice/fitting session.

Develop a system or approach that you thoroughly follow for every purchase and change in clubs; also develop an organized plan that will structure your budget and timeline for change. It's okay to make changes slowly and over a period of months or years, but develop and maintain an on-going improvement strategy that makes sense. Together with the assistance of a trusted PGA

Professional you can rebuild your bag as you also reshape your swing, step by step, and end up with significant leaps of improvement in your equipment and your skill level.

Keep in mind, customization of your clubs includes all 14 separate clubs. The professional you are working with might suggest starting your replacement of clubs with a different one than you were thinking of—perhaps your putter. Or adding a few hybrid clubs to your set make-up might be viewed as a necessary and significant way to accelerate your improvement and scoring. An evaluation of your game and current equipment as well as a conversation and strategy session is a necessary first step in developing an action plan centered on *your* objectives and goals. Spend the time and money up-front creating a comprehensive improvement plan with your professional. This procedure makes more sense than just going out and buying a new driver that looks good and is painted a cool color, or a club that a friend recently purchased and is claiming to be miraculous, or one that is being advertised on television with testimonials of playing professionals. This approach usually ends up costing more money and results in more frustration than it provides in genuine improvement and enjoyment playing the game.

Take advantage of the three outside components necessary to your improvement as a player—technological data, feedback and information; advancements in clubs, shafts, balls and other equipment; and the advice and expertise of a trusted golf professional. These are the same strategies that are also used by the best touring professionals around the world. Fortunately, they are readily available to almost all golfers who have the interest and dedication to pursue them.

Chapter 17 Practice

We have all heard the wise adage "practice with a purpose." In previous chapters there are sections devoted to practice ideas and drills related to specific club and shots, but that are mostly intended for use on the practice range. That kind of repetitive, focused practice is necessary and beneficial to develop physical regularity in your swing, but there are many other ways to practice and improve.

Play your regular course from different tee boxes: You will use a variety of clubs, shots and angles that are different from those you are accustomed to playing. Oftentimes this view of the course will give you a fresh perspective on new strategies you might employ when you return to your customary tees.

Use a short or old-fashioned carry bag set: Practice playing some holes with half of your current set. For example, use only your even numbered irons, one wedge and a few metal woods or hybrids. This set forces you to hit shots to distances with swings of less than full speed and swings of maximum speed. Also, you will need to create short shots with the clubs you are carrying that might be different than those you would normally use.

Walk 9 holes: Walking the course is good way to improve your overall health and will benefit your golf game in several ways. You will strengthen your leg muscles, work your cardio-vascular system and burn more calories. If possible, carry your clubs to enhance your work-out even further.

Join a golf league: Playing in a golf league that emphasizes a competitive golf environment and a friendly social atmosphere will heighten your effort level and golf focus. Look for leagues with good golfers who enjoy interacting with other serious golfers and who play at a high skill level. Leagues are usually structured with teams that play competitive matches each week against different opponents. The rounds are often played in a match play format that allows you to start over on each hole in a series of mini-matches inside of a bigger match. So, if you have a bad hole, you simply lose one point and the match is still competitive.

Watch golf on television: Watching televised golf is especially helpful during Sunday final rounds and major championships when everyone's effort level is at its highest. Do your viewing ***actively*** by participating in the same thinking and metal dilemmas the players are facing related to club and shot selection.

Watch the LPGA and Champions Tour on television: Model your swing after these players. Oftentimes the tempo, rhythm and fundamentals of their golf swings is nearly perfect and worthy of imitation.

Attend an event and watch advanced amateurs and/or professionals: Seeing great athletes play golf in person is humbling but can also be very motivating and instructive. It's always worth the price of admission and the trouble or inconvenience of traveling to and from the event.

Play different courses (and different types of courses): This engages your mind immediately and for prolonged stretches of time as you work your way around unfamiliar holes. It should also place different demands on your physical golf game.

Play a tournament or competitive event: Nothing will get your anxiety level higher and your nerves more activated than playing a stroke play tournament. If you prefer less stress and yet still want to force yourself to do your best, play in a fundraiser outing. Usually the format for these types of events is a scramble which is a comfortable blend of excitement, pressure and fun.

Play two balls: When the situation on the course permits, play some holes by yourself practicing with two balls. Most of the time, play your next pair of shots from the *better* of the first two balls by playing a second ball from that spot and just picking up the ball from the worst shot each time. Vary the distances of shots and practice from different lies to benefit more from your time. Just keep moving so you don't slow down other players and always repair both sets of divots and ball marks.

168

Practice extra putts: Again, when you are alone and the course is not crowded, putt out your first ball and then hit several other short putts (3-6 feet) from different locations, distances, and slopes. The variety of putts on every green is different and this is an efficient, valuable way to quickly practice your putting. Also, hit a long practice putt toward the edge of green and fringe at the side of the green you are leaving on the way back to your bag or cart. Try to stop the ball as close to the edge of the grasses as you can. These half dozen extra putts on every hole add up to many minutes of dreary rehearsals on the practice putting green and the variety of putting variables is unmatched.

Play two balls (variation 2): This time play the ball in the *worse* situation, not the better of the two situations. It's a great way to practice escape shots, shots from the rough, and shots that cause you to evaluate your options and decision making procedures when the situation is not easy and clearly apparent. This kind of practice will prepare you to select the proper shot options and keep you ready to play in competitive rounds.

Drop a ball in a bad spot: Deliberately drop a ball behind a tree, on the slope of ground near a water hazard, near the edge of a bunker or in a clump of particularly long grass and experience these unusual situations and shots while practicing on you own.

Play different shaped shots: Hit two balls from the same spot but try to shape each ball with different spin—right to left, left to right, higher than usual or lower than usual.

Practice in tough weather conditions: Try to hit the ball very solidly each time with a swing speed and effort of 75% of your maximum. Get used to playing with extra layer of clothing and make adjustments to club selection based on the temperature, humidity and wind.

Play with better players: No one wants to be embarrassed, but as your skills and abilities improve, the desire to compete and *keep-up* with better players in your group can motivate you to focus better, play better and score better. You will never know how good you can be until you test yourself against good competition.

Increase your fitness and activity level: Any exercise program, whether designed to improve flexibility, strength or aerobic or anaerobic conditioning, will help you improve your golf. Look into video and televised yoga or work-out programs for external structure and motivation. Add the old standards of taking the stairs, parking further out in a parking lot, and walking throughout the day as ways you can easily increase your activity level and improve your overall conditioning, even while working or running errands.

Develop healthy routines in as many aspects of your life as possible. Become more dedicated to proper sleep, nutrition, fitness and practice throughout the week and repeat these good habits month after month. Improving your health over the long run will improve your golf game and your quality of life.

Chapter 18 The PGA of America: How to Select the Right Professional for You

No matter where you live in the United States you can find a certified Class A, PGA Golf Professional. The PGA website can easily help you locate the certified professionals in your area. Also, the good, old-fashioned word-of-mouth method is an effective way to not only find out who is in your area, but additionally, hear other golfers' opinions about local professionals.

Becoming a PGA Professional is a slow, comprehensive and exhausting process. In order to simply begin the PGA Apprentice Program, the first step in becoming a certified professional, an interested person must first pass the Playing Ability Test (PAT).

The PAT is a sanctioned event with tournament directors and rules officials that is played strictly under the Rules of Golf in every section of the PGA throughout the year. The competitors play 36 holes in one day, two consecutive 18 hole rounds, on the same golf course with the other test applicants. Any of the players who score at or below a pre-determined cut-off score pass the test; the passing score is usually an aggregate total near 150 strokes (75, 75 for the two rounds) or less depending on the slope and difficulty of the course. The PAT is a required entrance point into the PGA Professional Golf Management Program for people pursuing a career as a golf professional.

Applicants must then apprentice under the mentorship of a PGA Class A Professional by working full time for a period of at least 36 months. This work experience portion of the program is coupled with three distinct levels of academic courses of study in approximately 25 separate knowledge areas related to the golf business. This educational portion of the program includes comprehensive testing at three different times of the study process which correspond to the three levels of the apprentice. Courses include such topics as accounting, merchandising, supervision of employees, golf instruction, the rules of golf, golf cart fleet management and professional business writing to name a few.

Statistics over the years of the program show that less than 50% of the people who start the program ever become fully certified by the PGA of America as a Class A Professional. So, generally speaking, you can feel good about the knowledge, experience and expertise of a PGA Professional when you begin your search. However, people are people, and there are other elements to consider in order to find a compatible professional for you.

Let's examine some personal criteria worthy of your consideration as you enter the selection process:

Personality: Stop by to meet the professional and discuss your needs, or at least, call the person on the telephone. You can tell quite a bit about someone's personality and friendliness in just a few minutes. Obviously, when you finish the conversation you should feel like you want to spend more time working with this person on your swing and/or equipment needs.

Availability and Flexibility: Verify that the PGA Professional is willing to work around *your* schedule and not the other way around. Also ask if you can meet with them during evenings or on weekends. This is also a good time to inquire about their cancellation policy. The working relationship is a *two-way street* and you should feel there is a proper balance between you two in working around each other's life demands.

Professionalism: Try to garner an impression of the professional's business approach and maturity through his/her dress and appearance. More importantly, listen closely to the person's ideas, the type of language the person uses and how well the person expressed his/her ideas. Also, note whether or not the person was punctual and on-time—this respect for each other's time should be mutual.

Teaching Style: Ask the PGA Professional to describe his/her instructional approach by explaining to you how a series of three lessons would be structured. Listen for a logical plan that covers the topics you are interested in and determine if these lessons would provide you with a cost-effective path to improvement. Other things to listen for include warm-up time, location and length of the lessons (for instance will you ever practice on the actual golf course), the variety of activities, descriptions of his/her teaching style, use of technology and the recommended time frame and frequency of follow-up lessons. If any elements of this conversation don't matchup with your goals and objectives, you should delay scheduling a formal appointment until you have more time to think over what was discussed before making a commitment to move forward.

Quality of the Facility: Ask to see the practice facility so that you can assess its overall quality and variety of instructional settings. Look at the condition of the practice balls, whether there are grass tees, a separate teaching area, any instructional equipment or teaching aids and special areas such as practice bunkers and a practice green.

Knowledgeable and Helpful: Try to determine from the time you spend with the PGA Professional if he/she has good ideas and has enough life and teaching experience to share them effectively with you. The person must be able to explain concepts and techniques in a way that make sense to you and that you can easily implement in your game.

Use of Technology: If you are interested in technical data related to your golf swing are these options available? Also, does the professional have the capability to take video of your swing using computer analysis software, and to share the video and analysis results with you? If so, what are the associated costs of these services?

Assistance with New Equipment: If this is an area of interest for you, check with the professional regarding his/her knowledge base regarding the latest clubs and shafts. Also, find out if the facility has *fitting carts* by the club manufacturers you have an interest in testing and whether the facility is scheduled to host a *Demo Day* during the season and if your favorite manufacturers will be participating in the event.

Loyalty and Longevity: It is fair to discuss loyalty programs and discounts with the PGA Professional if you are contemplating a long term business relationship. Ask about existing programs related to blocks of lessons or multi-club purchase. For example, if you pre-book one lesson/month for the entire six to eight months of the season, does the professional offer a discounted rate. Or if you purchase equipment from the golf shop, will the professional help you with the transition from your old club to the new club, by perhaps spending some time on the driving range with you to help find the proper setting for your new adjustable driver.

Do You Feel Welcome? It's a basic business principle but make sure you simply feel good in the person's company and feel respected by the PGA Professional. Sometimes common sense and decency are rare qualities that are hard to find. You are the customer, so make sure you have a high enough level of confidence in the professional that you are willing to entrust him/her with the development of your game.

Acknowledgements

I would like to thank my publisher, Summit Classic Press, for the continued confidence in me expressed in the willingness to publish this book and for the editorial and technical assistance provided throughout the process. I am proud to have this title among the other quality books of Summit Classic Press.

Several people have been instrumental in assisting and mentoring me in the golf business. I owe a debt of gratitude to Frank Cisterino, PGA, Herb Page, PGA and Trent Maxwell, PGA for the opportunities they gave me and for their encouragement and guidance over the years. I am also grateful to the staff of the Northern Ohio Section of the PGA of America, and especially to Dominic Antenucci, PGA.

Moreover, thanks to my friends and coworkers at Windmill Lakes Golf Club, Candywood Golf Club and Avalon Lakes Golf and Country Club. We've spent many hours together and I've enjoyed the good times and the experiences we've shared. Also, thanks to Drs. Candella and Mrs. Candella for the opportunities they've given to me. I truly appreciate the confidence Ron Klingle, Adam Scott and Nick Dinsmore from Avalon Golf and Country Club have demonstrated in giving me the opportunity to work as a Golf Instructor at that marvelous facility. I appreciate the friendships I have among all of the dedicated individuals at Avalon GCC, and I am honored to work in their company.

Special thanks to James Bandy for the suggestion of the need for a book specifically intended for the left-handed golfer, and to Steve Pugh for his willingness to be the golfer in the photos that appear in this book.

My students over the years have taught me so much and made me a better instructor—I can't thank them enough for their loyalty and for sharing their insights. You all inspire me to learn more about this marvelous game and to pass on my ideas to other interested golfers.

Finally, I would like to extend a very special thanks to my family for their unwavering support and encouragement over the years.

Author Biography

Warne Palmer is a Class A PGA Golf Professional in the Northern Ohio Section of the PGA of America. This book is the culmination of his forty years of experience as a golf professional and educator.

Currently, he is an Instructor of Golf at Avalon Golf and Country Club in Warren, Ohio.

He is also the author of *Palmer 60/40 Golf: Modern Golf Swing Fundamentals*.

Visit the **Summit Classic Press** website at
www.summitclassicpress.com
for information about other available books, our schedule of
upcoming new releases, and information about book design and
publishing services

Summit Classic Press
265 South Main St., Suite 115
Akron, Ohio 44308

Printed in Great Britain
by Amazon

32835927R00108